Welcome Cornwall Coliseum

The Venue that we all loved, as remembered by the fans, the staff and some of the bands that played there...

By Ian Carroll (CCA*)

* Cornwall Coliseum Addict

Dedicated to my ever loving & extremely understanding, wife the lovely Raine and my three sons, Nathan, Joshua & Rex

Also thanks to my keenest and most avid other supporter –
'Laura McCartney,
for her continued encouragement.
Thank you also for all your support and help friends on Facebook and Twitter

Thank you for supporting the hard work of this author

Introduction

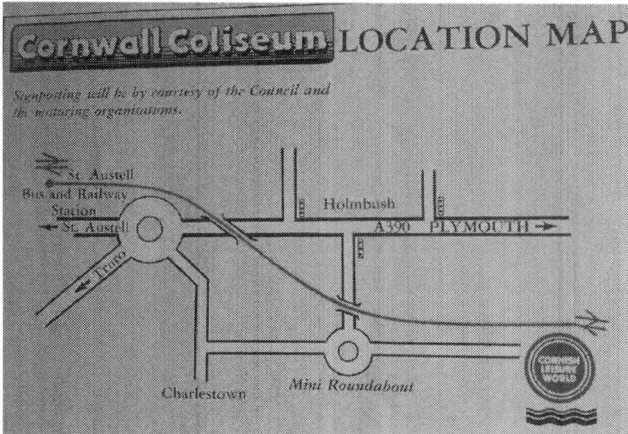

From when I was very young at Primary School I loved music. Music was a great passion for me, I always remember me and my friend Gary Nowell memorising the words to the latest chart hits, as they printed a whole songs lyrics each week in 'Weekend' magazine, which both our parents bought.

My father liked music, as did my mother, but their respective record collections contained many 'classical albums' (my fathers) and Bill Haley 78's (my mothers) and the only records that held any interest with me were the Beatles ones (my fathers again), which I still have to this day.

The only other records we had were film soundtracks played by the Geoff Love Orchestra, so not even the original artists. When it was time for Sunday lunch we would listen to the 'Larry The Lamb' album, which my sister thrived on as she was seven years younger than me and loved it.

So how I ended up with such a vast and diverse taste in music is beyond me; perhaps I was rebelling against my parents lack of musical taste and filling it with every style I could, though rock and heavy metal were the musical styles that I started to listen to most as I made my progress through Secondary School.

As I neared the end of my academic career I decided that I wanted to attend as many acts/gigs/festivals as possible and so a trip to St Austell was the nearest venue that was host to international stars.

Cornwall Coliseum was the venue of my first ever gig – Tygers Of Pan Tang, Magnum and Alkatrazz in 1981 when I was still at school and I went on to go another forty three times as well seeing all the big bands of the time:

Whitesnake x3 Gillan x2 Rainbow x2 Magnum x3 Ramones   KISS Billy Connolly Waterboys Thin Lizzy x2 Japan Gary Numan   Belinda Carlisle x2 Hazel O'Connor Saxon x2   Black Sabbath x2 Robert Plant Status Quo Public Image Ltd Elton John   Shamen EMF / PWE The Damned Motorhead East 1 Iron Maiden Big Country Ultravox Slade Terrorvision The Alarm Dio Marillion UB40

So, although I'm from Devon, support the 'ONLY' football team in the county (Green Army) and only visit Cornwall for trips to the beach and gigs, I have quite an affinity to the venue that is no longer.

I visited the site on 29th April, to say goodbye to a place that I had spent, but not wasted, most of my youth at and it was sad to see what remained of the venue. I have since been back on 16th June and sadly the whole shell of the building is now gone and all that remains is a vast empty, sandy space.

After the Coliseum went into decline I had to travel much further afield to Bristol, Exeter and quite often to London for gigs.

My festival calendar for most summers is still quite busy and this year was my 29th Reading Festival – I wrote their 'Official' book and now write for their website as well, so my passion for music still carries on, even though I have now hit the big 50.

So, I leave it to you all to sit back and enjoy the highlights, the memories and the 'crazy crazy nights' spent at a little venue with a huge heart on Crinnis beach in Carlyon Bay.

I'll let the picture do the talking…

Cornwall Coliseum

Carlyon Bay • St. Austell
Cornwall • PL25 3RD
Telephone: Par (072681) 4261
Fax: (072681) 7231

General Manager: Paul Higgins

December 1990

TECHNICAL INFORMATION

Capacity:	Seated with 30ft deep stage:	2196
	Seated with 24ft deep stage:	(variable) 2306
	Arena (standing) + balconies (seated)	3326
Loading:	Direct onto stage	
Staging:	56 x 38 x 4 maximum x PA wings	
Barrier:	Fixed to stage (Arena/standing shows)	
Lighting:	4 winched lighting bars (2 foh), side booms	
	3 winched scenery bars	
Power:	3 x 315 amps	
	3 x 125 amps	
	1 x 160 amps	
	3 x 32 amp winch	
Spotlights:	Xenon Supertroupers (2)	
	75ft from stage (approx.)	
Mixer/Sound Positions:	75ft from stage (movable)	
PA Wings:	Max. 13 x 20 stage right	
	13 x 12 stage left	
Dressing Rooms:	4 with showers/toilets. Heated.	
	Also Catering Cabin available.	
Production Office:	Direct telephone (0726) 814 973	

The Crew:		
	General Manager	— Paul Higgins
	Deputy General Manager	—
	Box Office Manager	— Sallie Bragg
	Stage Manager	— (OTC Stage Services) Barrie Honeyman
	Electrician	— Nigel Scott
	Security	— Murray Hawkey
	Press/P.A.	— Pat Barnes
	Promotions	— Terry Tonkin/Pam Sekula

A Brief Potted History of the Cornwall Coliseum

So 'our' venue is now gone. A dusty space next to Crinnis Beach on Carlyon Bay and all we have are our memories and this book. A timeline is the best way to describe how the venue/site went from success to decline to nothing, so read on.

- The Prince of Wales visited the area and suggested that a sports club could perhaps be built next to the beach for the local wealthy businessmen and families.
- In the 1930's the Riviera Club opened on the site – Edward VIII and Mrs Simpson were rumoured to be amongst the visitors who used the venue.
- During World War II the beach was used for military manoeuvers and the completion and development of the site was put on hold until the war had passed.
- 1950's the site re-opens and continues to build in popularity.
- The venue was bought by Mr & Mrs Lovett and they started to use it as a 'seated' concert venue with 2000 able to attend; the whole complex became known as the New Cornish Riviera Lido, the music venue was still called the Riviera Club as it had always been known.
- The Riviera Club rose in popularity with many of the bands that were in the charts at the time selling out concerts at the venue
- Dances were organized for the venue and once again proved incredibly popular in the 1960's
- Through the 70's and 80's and the 'Punk & New Wave Revolution' the venue began to thrive, with the popularity of 'Rock & Metal' as well, the venue became a major venue on most bands touring schedules.
- The original badminton courts were converted into Beelzebub's Nightclub – the nightclub would go through

several name changes over the years and would become Bentleys, then Quasars and finally changing its name to Gossips.

- The site made additions with the Wimpy restaurant, the amusement arcade and the very popular 'roller disco'.
- Complex changed its name to Cornish Leisure World
- Complex changed its name once more and for the final time to Cornwall Coliseum.
- The venue was the largest of its kind in the South West – 3,400 standing and 2,600 seated for concerts.
- Every band who were popular in the day lined up to play the venue including – Paul McCartney, The Clash, Genesis, The Who, KISS, Iron Maiden, Black Sabbath, Japan, Depeche Mode, The Cure, Sir Cliff Richard, Elton John, Bon Jovi, The Jam, The Ramones, Whitesnake, Rainbow, UB40, Thin Lizzy, Magnum, The Specials, Madness, Belinda Carlisle, Billy Connolly, Gillan, Ozzy Osbourne, Slade, The Alarm, Page & Plant, The Damned, Motorhead, 10cc, Roy Orbison, Scorpions, Saxon, Duran Duran, ABC, Tina Turner, Status Quo, Hawkwind, Bucks Fizz, Tom Jones, Wham!, The Commodores, Gary Numan, Shakin' Stevens, OMD, Marillion, Sade and hundreds and hundreds more
- 1986 – Alison Moyet makes the venue for 'Is This Love?' at the complex and on the beach
- 1988 – T'Pau record some of their video for 'Road To Our Dream' at the venue
- 1990 – Planning permission was applied for to build an extension to the Coliseum and luxury houses, but never came to fruition
- 1991 – The Plymouth Pavilions opens with Extreme playing as one of the first concerts and bands tend to bypass the Coliseum due to the distance factor.
- Concerts begin to dwindle and popularity of the venue with promoters with it.
- 1999 – Gary Barlow sells a rumoured 80 tickets to a show at the venue and tickets are given away to friends and family of the Coliseum to try and bulk out the crowd.
- The venue had some smaller shows upstairs from the Wimpy which was originally the amusement arcade – one of the final shows (and the last one I attended) was Terrovision in 2000
- The venue eventually closed completely with Gossips nightclub closing as well for the final time in 2003

- 2015 – April demolition begins on the site
- 2015 – July the Cornwall Coliseum is no more...

The 1960's

"We were called The Cosmonauts and based near St Austell.
We were billed as Cornwall's youngest group, our ages ranging
from 11 to 16. We played all over Cornwall and auditioned for
Opportunity Knocks but didn't get on...
However in July '66 we got on the support bill for Chris Farlowe
and The Thunderbirds at the Coliseum, or the 'Riviera Club' as it
was known then. He was number one then with Out of Time. At the
end of the evening the drummer let me play his drums...I was 12...
What an experience for a kid."
Chris Gray (The Cosmonauts – Drums)

"My earliest memories of Cornwall Coliseum go back to around
1960, there used to dance nights with proper live dance bands. My
parents used to take us there, they were wonderful dancers, and
we would sit and watch them. This is probably where I got my love
of live music from; sadly I still have two left feet. As a very young
teenager, not old enough to drive I had an evening job collecting
and washing glasses, I was lucky enough to be chauffeured to and
fro by Bill Martin and Malcolm Stanaway."
Shirley Penrose (Fowey, Cornwall)

"My only regret is that the Beatles never played there. They are my
favourite all time group, for the simple reason that they were the
last group I heard before I lost my hearing (due to meningitis)."
Stephen Nott (St Austell, Cornwall)

"Remember it well from mid to late 60's including the carousel.

I used to go in the swimming pool just about every day in school holidays, the cost to get in was 1 shilling and sixpence (7 and a half pence today).

Quite often shared changing rooms with the wrestlers that would be 'practising' routines in the main hall for the weekly wrestling shows. Remember seeing the wrestling stars of the day there: Jackie Pallo, Honey Boy Zimba and Mick McManus amongst others.

Getting into the pool early morning was a priority as a quick walk around it would reveal coins on the bottom, thus being able to recoup my entrance money before others arrived."

Wally Whale (Cornwall)

"All I can recall was being thrown out after we worked out how to beat the bandits that were there.

Spent many a good day down there, miss the old Wimpy shop.

I also remember wrestling being on at one stage plus in the early days a concert was put on by Procol Harum."

Paul Coon (St Austell, Cornwall)

I remember the carousel well and yes, it was used, I rode on it many times.

I think it belonged to the Lovett's. There were one armed bandits, a ghost train and other things.

Crinnis was my second home all summer as a child. I went every day into my teenage years.

Some of the wrestling evenings were all male, black tie and very posh!"

Amanda Mabley (Wadebridge, Cornwall)

"I went to see The Pretty Things play here back in the 1960's (can't remember exactly but '65 or '66 would probably be about right) they were touring Cornwall at the time and we liked them so much we went to see them at The Blue Lagoon in Newquay a few days later."

Simon Robinson (Falmouth, Cornwall)

"In my teens I want to see Herman's Hermits ... Slightly unimpressed, as I was more into folk at the time. I really didn't get the screaming."

France's Deacon (Truro, Cornwall)

The Early 1970's

"I remember going inside the Coliseum as a kid (1970'ish) and there was a beautiful carousel on display. I can't remember if it was used or not, I certainly didn't have a ride."
Helen Wilson (St Austell, Cornwall)

"I was fortunate to experience the Coliseum in the 1970's when it was the 'Cornish Riviera Lido' when the Lovell family owned it. My Grandmother worked in the gift shop during the summer season and both my parents worked there part time in the busy summer holidays. Both my sister and I would spend every weekend there whilst our parents worked. We were young, my sister was about 11 and I was 7. We would spend hours exploring and would be away for what seemed to be hours at a time. It was a safe place and in all the years we spent there no one ever approached us in anyway.
At the end of the car park furthest from the building was a forest of bamboos growing and off to one side an old war time 'Pill box' look out hut, which was always full of beer cans and smelt of pee!! We would chase around the bamboos and climb on the pillbox and occasionally venture inside, but never staying in there long!!
In the middle of the car park was a house, which was known to us as 'Angela's house'. I'm not sure exactly why it was called this as no one lived there and it was just used as storage and keeping a few hundred blue bottle fly's in. We used to say it was haunted and dare each other to look through the windows to see if anyone was in there.
Around the arcade at the front of the building we would always find 'spent' gun cartridges, to this day we don't know why they where there??
The arcade was managed by a guy called Ernie Ford, a big jolly man who lived in a small building alongside the showman

caravans that adorned the rear of the building. As kids we would play with his children and the other children from families that worked there. It was an amazing community at the time. Ernie would call us over and tell us to cup our hands, and then would fill them with pennies and tell us to play the machines to 'test' them.

In the back of the building, was home to the Victorian merry-go-round and the ghost train. I remember the owner's son, Jonathon, would dress up and hide in the ghost train and scare the life out of people on the ride. I remember 'Paper Lace' was in the charts at the time with 'The Night Chicago Died', which always seemed to be playing over the music system there.

My Mum worked in the gift shop with my Gran and my Dad worked as a pool attendant. One weekend he saved the life of a young boy who jumped in the deep end of the pool with a mouth full of crisps, and promptly sank. It took Dad two or three attempts to pull him out. He did and the boy lived to see another day.

I was sad when the Lovell family sold the business and my Grandmother changed her job and started working somewhere else. It would be a few years before I saw the Coliseum again."

Iain Armstrong (Whitstone, North Cornwall)

1973

The year began with the UK, Denmark and the Republic of Ireland entering the European Union, Richard Nixon was sworn into office for his second term in the USA and the US involvement in Vietnam came to an end.

In the wonderful world of entertainment Aerosmith and the New York Dolls released their debut albums, Elvis Presley's concert from Hawaii was broadcast worldwide and gained more viewers than the moon landings by Apollo crew, Pink Floyd released 'The Dark Side of the Moon and 'The Godfather' won the Best Picture Oscar at the Academy Awards.

The Watergate Scandal rocked the US, the first 'mobile' phone was introduced, Spurs won the League Cup beating Norwich 1-0 and Sunderland beat Leeds United in the FA Cup final, the World Trade Centre (the Twin Towers) opened in New York, the Sears Tower opened in Chicago, the DEA (Drug Enforcement Agency) was founded in the US and the 'Three Day Week' was introduced in the UK to limit electrical consumption – TV channels had to finish their broadcasting at 10:30pm each day.

This year saw the passing of Noel Coward, Edward G. Robinson, Pablo Picasso, Irene Ryan (Granny in 'The Beverly Hillbillies), Betty Grable, Veronica Lake, J.R.R. Tolkien, Robert Ryan and the Kung Fu movie legend and founder of Jeet Kune Do – Bruce Lee at the age of only 32.
Jim Parsons of 'The Big Bang Theory' was born this year, as well as David Draiman (Disturbed), Pharrell Williams, Adrien Brody, Dermot O'Leary, Josh Homme (Queens of the Stone Age), Heidi Klum, Neil Patrick Harris, Peter Kay, Ryan Giggs and the man that invented a product that we all use a great deal everyday Larry Page (co-founder of Google).

The biggest selling single of the year was 'Tie A Yellow Ribbon Round the Ole Oak Tree' by Dawn and the Christmas Number One was the ULTIMATE Christmas song of all time 'Merry Christmas Everybody' by Slade, still a favourite every year at Christmas to this day, with several re-issues also getting into the charts most years.

"Hoping my memory serves me well…
I believe we played the first time down in this area in 1973, 3 hits under my belt, well attended, but nobody expected the craziness of the fans! When the fight broke out at the Coliseum during my show, I had no choice; there were no bouncers to speak of so to diffuse the situation I simply carried on.
Hard to keep fighting when 'Can The Can' is blaring over the P.A., it's such a feel good song!"

Suzi Quatro (Vocals/Bass)

"I'm from Falmouth and as a child my mum took me there many times for the beach, because it had many things to occupy both children and adults alike!
It was a 'mini' theme park in itself and considering its size, there couldn't be too many places like it in the world. I remember swimming in the outdoor pool, the monorail, crazy golf etc. besides swimming in the water too! Not forgetting the arcade. I had so much fun there and one could never be bored.
It also had eating establishments like fish 'n' chips and a burger joint etc."

Gary Cocks (Falmouth, Cornwall)

1976

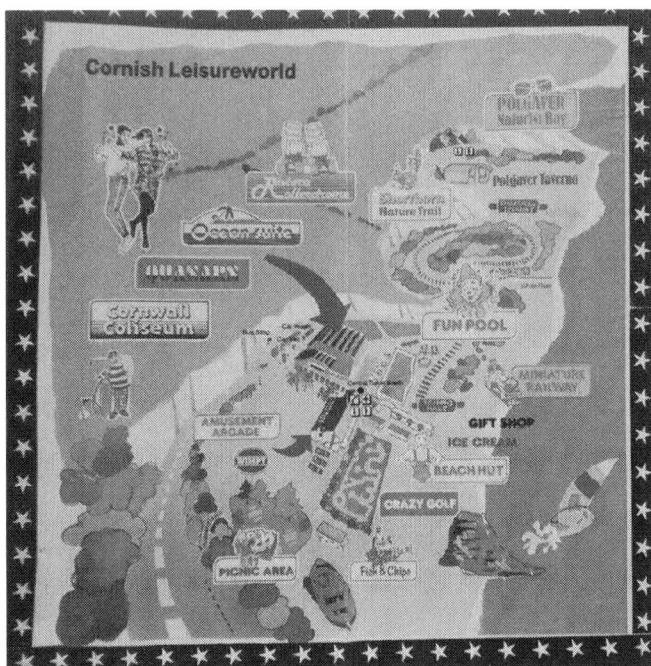

Cornish Leisureworld

*T*he year began with the first commercial flight of the Concorde, the Scottish Labour Party was formed and the Provisional IRA set off several bombs in London's West End. The year carried on with the resignation of Harold Wilson and his replacement James Callaghan taking over as Prime Minister, Patty Hearst was found guilty of a bank heist in San Francisco, the Intercity 125 HST train was introduced, Ford launched the Fiesta and the Apple Computer Company was formed by Steve Jobs and Steve Wozniak.

In music, the classic album 'Frampton Comes Alive!' was released, U2 formed, Bob Marley was involved in an assassination attempt in Jamaica, the Sex Pistols swore a lot on the Bill Grundy show on TV, the Eagles released the classic album 'Hotel California', Stevie Wonder released 'Songs In The Key Of Life'; the Ramones released their self-titled album and played their first professional show at CBGB's in New York.

Many famous deaths happened throughout the year including Agatha Christie, Alistair Sim, Field Marshall Montgomery, Howard Hughes and Chairman Mao. In addition many celebrities were born including Emma Bunton (Baby Spice), Isla Fisher, Reese Witherspoon, Colin Farrell, Benedict Cumberbatch, Ryan Reynolds and Shagrath lead singer of the Norwegian 'Black Metal' band Dimmu Borgir.

The Christmas Number One spot was held by Johnny Mathis with 'When A Child Is Born' and the biggest selling single of the year was by The Brotherhood of Man with their Eurovision Song Contest winning song 'Save All Your Kisses For Me.'

"As for me and my memories I really wouldn't know where to begin ... or end. I'd finished University when my father bought the site in 1976.
It was never just a beach or a venue or a work place to me, it was my everything for the seven or eight years I worked there - even my home for a couple of seasons.
As a family business, we took on a beach and a building containing an indoor fairground and turned it into a major entertainment and concert venue.
I spent most of my twenties there."

Ali McNally (Sidmouth, Devon)

"Back in the late 1970's and early 1980's, there were a few venues in the South West where we could see the bands of the day.
Torquay had the Town Hall and the Pavilion, Plymouth had the Guildhall and the Van Dyke and Cornwall had the Coliseum.
Sure, it meant a drive down from Torbay, but it was well worth the trip to St Austell to visit this fantastic venue for the evening. Fitted out with what was said to be the longest bar in the country, one never needed to go thirsty during a gig, as there was always a space at the bar where you could be served. Drinks were certainly needed in the hot and heavy atmosphere within as the aroma of Patchouli oil (+ others!) wafted around in the smoke filled room!!

Standing was always the order of the day back then, no seating and no crash barriers to keep us back from the stage – happy days.

I cannot remember there ever being any trouble either, despite the easy-going atmosphere of the time.

Fond memories of seeing great acts such as Status Quo (at least 8 times there) plus Rory Gallagher, Hawkwind, Motorhead, Slade and many more. I wish now I had seen some of the other big names that played there.

The drive home always flew past as our ears were ringing with the booming sounds from the custom built Marshall speakers that they all used!" **Derek**

Hore (Paignton, Devon)

"Well where to begin?!

My very first memory must have been in around 1976 going to fireworks night. I was only 7 and we had newly moved to Cornwall. Fantastic fireworks, but one of them scared me and I ran off - bumped into my dad's new boss (luckily!) who reunited me with my parents."

Alison Pearson (Nr Exeter, Devon)

"I went to see Leo Sayer at the the Cornwall Coliseum, it was out first big concert. He sang 'You Make Me Feel Like Dancing'. Very energetic and a very good night, but it took us as long getting from the venue to the main road for the trip home!

We also saw Gilbert O'Sullivan and he was very good too."

Rose Francis (Plymouth, Devon)

1977

*T*he year began with the introduction of the Apple Computer, Gary Gilmore was the first person to be executed by firing squad in Utah after the reintroduction of the death penalty, the first space shuttle 'Enterprise' did its first test flight and Jimmy Carter was sworn in as the 39th President of the United States succeeding Gerald Ford.

In the world of entertainment the TV series 'Roots' covering the story from the beginning to end of the slave trade in the US began broadcasting, Fleetwood Mac released their classic album 'Rumours', the Sex Pistols released 'Never Mind The Bollocks' and Space Mountain opened at Disneyworld.

In sport, Red Rum won his 3rd Grand National and Virginia Wade stormed to victory winning Wimbledon (in what was also the Queen's Silver Jubliee year).

Born this year were Michael Fassbender, Sarah Michelle Gellar, Tom Hardy, Orlando Bloom, Shakira and Kanye West. The world of music and entertainment lost several legends including Elvis Presley, Bing Crosby, Groucho Marx, Joan Crawford, Marc Bolan, members of the US southern rock band Lynyrd Skynyrd and William Castle - film director/producer of such greats as 'The House On Haunted Hill', 'The Tingler' and 'Rosemary's Baby'.

The biggest selling single of the year and the Christmas No.1 was a 'double whammy' for Paul McCartney and Wings with 'Mull Of Kintyre'.

"I first started working in what was to become known as the Cornwall Coliseum, in the summer of 1977.
I was about to start an Art Foundation Course, at Cornwall Tech in

September and needed a job to fill in the time, and earn some pocket money.

Little did I know that I'd still be working there part time, six years later.

My first summer was spent working behind the bars. Mainly in the front bar (sometimes known as the Beach Bar), and the bar in Beelzebub's Disco. I would occasionally work in the ballroom bar (later to become the Ocean Suite), for functions or the occasional local band, like Frank Yonco.

It was also during this time that I got to know the McNally family.

It was Ross and Heather, the younger two of the four siblings I met first, and towards the end of the season, we and a couple of others, went to Plymouth to see the Sex Pistols, whilst they were on their "undercover" SPOT (Sex Pistols on Tour) tour. We were into Punk and New Wave at the time.

It was at this time, whilst in Beelzebub's one night, pogoing to some punk track, that Bar Manager Gerry Trevartha walked in, and said the now immortal words "Look! It's Skippy the Bush Kangaroo!" From that day onwards, I would henceforth be known as 'Skippy'. A name, that many still know me by, to this day.

I remember the early part of the summer season being quiet at times, as the weather was not that good. So, being a member of the seasonal casual staff, there were often days when I was sent home, as there was no work for me.

As the weather improved, my hours picked up, until the week of the Radio 1 Roadshow, when my hours exceeded 100 in just one week. Even though I was only being paid around 69p an hour, it went a long way in 1977, where a pint of bitter was about 29p a pint, lager was 30p a pint and strong lager, just 32p a pint.

Once I started at college, I continued to work some evenings and weekends, throughout the autumn and winter months."

Martyn (aka Skippy) Feather (Lancing, Sussex)

"I worked at the venue as a 'Bouncer" (all areas, including Roller Blade, Concerts, Disco, Functions) for around two-three years after having worked at Reading Festival doing Stage/Back-Stage Security in 1977.

I also worked there as a Kitchen hand, Cellar hand, and various other guises as a teenager. There was also a stand alone cafe across the car-park to the South on the cliff side."

Clive Rodell (Sydney, Australia)

"I remember the carousel too. There was a ghost train in there at

the same time, and me and my mates walked through it as there was nobody in there to stop us!!

Mike Bennett (Cornwall)

CORNISH LEISURE WORLD — CARLYON BAY, ST AUSTELL SOUTH CORNWALL — PAR 4004

Cornwall Coliseum

The South-West's major concert hall and arena presenting international stars of entertainment and sport. 15,000 sq ft plus balconies. Capacities 3,300 for a standing show or 2,500 for a seated show.

10,000 sq ft of indoor rink for family skating.

Cornwall's premier nightspot. Sensational sounds and lights with the best and latest music.

Function room with restaurant right on the beach. Ideal for weddings, dinner dances or seminars.

CARLYON BAY — 1½ miles of sandy bays & beaches. Three years winners of the EEC Blue Flag Award for clean beaches. Naturist beach forms part of the 77-acre site.

JUST A BITE — Fast food restaurant and take-away service. Hot & cold drinks, burgers and grills, delicious desserts.

A great range of the very latest electronic video games, pinball machines, and pool tables.

FACTS AND FIGURES: The 25,000 sq ft of exhibition space is part of a 55,000 sq ft complex.

Parking for over 2,000 cars.

St. Austell is centrally located and is the largest conurbation in Cornwall with population within a 15 mile radius of 150,000 and within a 30 mile radius of 550,000.

We have the back-up of a fully professional management team and any type of show, event, exhibition or conference is catered for. Box Office facilities, telext message centre, fax etc all available.

1978

Film Director Roman Polanski fled to France because of an underage sex scandal, US serial killer Ted Bundy was caught, Larry Flynt – owner and publisher of 'Hustler' was shot and paralysed, Louise Brown the UK's first 'test tube' baby was born, Pope John Paul I dies after being Pope for only 33 days, the 'Son Of Sam' serial killer in the USA David Berkowitz was jailed for 365 years and the Chicago serial killer John Wayne Gacy was arrested.

Kate Bush hit the number 1 position with her debut single 'Wuthering Heights', Izhar Cohen & The Alphabeta won Eurovision with 'A-Ba-Ni-Bi', 'Dallas premiered on TV, Argentina won the Fifa World Cup and the movies 'Superman' starring Christopher Reeves and 'Grease' with John Travolta and Olivia Newton John were released at the cinema.

The world of the movies lost cult film director Ed Wood and Robert Shaw (from 'Jaws') and television lost Will Geer (Grandpa Walton). Ashton Kutcher was born, so was Claudio Sanchez of Coheed and Cambria, James Franco, Andy Samberg, James Corden and Kobe Bryant.

The Number One Christmas single was 'Mary's Boy Child' and the best selling single of the year was 'Rivers of Babylon / Brown Girl In The Ring' both by Boney M.

"I continued working behind the bars for much of the start of 1978, and even had my 21st Birthday party in Beelzebub's. Graham McNally kindly let me have the use of the nightclub free of charge, as long as I (or should I say my parents) paid for the buffet, and Andy Munro was DJ at the time, and as a friend, he offered to DJ free of charge too.
I continued working at New Cornish Riviera Lido, until I went to college at Bristol Polytechnic in September 1978.

Whenever I returned home from college for the holidays, I'd persuade them to take me back on for a few weeks."
Martyn (aka Skippy) Feather (Lancing, Sussex)

"I returned again in the late seventies as part of the cleaning team and spent many happy hours cleaning up after the shows and the daily rounds of the Ocean Suite, many times chasing the pool guys with their wet feet on a freshly waxed floor, The Wimpy and Amusement arcade, juke box on the Police belting out, I did a summer season in the arcade."
Shirley Penrose (Fowey, Cornwall)

"My parents wouldn't let me go to Sham 69 gig but I said I was going to stay at my friends house and she said she was staying at mine because she wasn't allowed to go either, trouble is my mum rang my friends Mum about something and they found out, we were at the concert and my Dad and her Dad came and dragged us out.
Was grounded for a month he he."
Nicola Toms (Lanlivery, Cornwall)

Very hostile crowd.
Drinks etc. flying thru the air along with lots of spit.
The Lurkers came on and played a few songs accompanied by everything being chucked at them and spat at. Band went off for Graham McNally to come to the mike asking for calm and threaten that the band would not come back on if things didn't calm down.
Then in the lights you saw this big glob of spit flying thru the air to hit Graham square in the face, it was like in slow motion. He went off and the group came back on.
During a song the drummer saw a fan climbing onto the stage. In a flash this great big muscled drummer threw his sticks down and ran over to punch him into oblivion and smacked the stage climber back into the crowd. Lol!
It was unforgettable!! Needless to say the group went off and never came back on.
Gary Warne (St Austell)

"In later years, I continued to use the place such as the concert venue.
Although I can't recall exact dates or even years, I saw Adam and the Ants twice, Status Quo (fab show), Five Star, Darts (great live band) Showaddywaddy, Hawkwind (Ginger Baker was guest

drummer - Levitation tour) and the great Paul McCartney (WOW)."

Gary Cocks (Falmouth, Cornwall)

"They had fireworks every year. Went in the late 70's and it was wet and all the fireworks were not going in the right directions; I think a few hit the crowd. It was a disaster and we never went again."

Robert Adams (St Austell)

"In Memory of my dad Terry Cross.
My dad Terry, worked at the resort known over the years as: Cornish Riviera, Carlyon Bay, Cornish Coliseum and other names; from the mid 1970's until his death in 1978 aged 36.
\He was on the maintenance side of the resort. As a builder and carpenter he undertook most of the building work whilst he worked there. He was also known as a funny man and well liked man...and a storyteller supreme.
His workshop was the white building in the far corner of the resort

by the forever steps, (as they felt when you climbed them, even when drunk, it was an easier option to walk up the long windy hill of an entrance) same end as the "Dracula" shipwreck.

I basically had my first 7 years of my life there: memories of my dad working, the smell of wood chippings, the ice creams on hot days, playing crazy golf on quiet days, playing on the beach with my mate Becky (daughter of then owners "Uncle" Graham and "Auntie" Angela) the can's of fizzy drink that were stored in the back of the workshop (that's a secret by the way...we'd not paid for them). The day he built my hobbyhorse and I rode it there for the first time.

The most scary day of my then short life...the shipwreck appearance. Being told it was for a film about some "not so nice fella" called "Dracula" (did my love of vampires start then? I wonder).

Going into the big hall where my dad had built the new offices and listening to Kate Bush "Babushka" on the radio whilst he worked (not knowing he'd soon not be working anymore).

Walking around the innards of place, during all hours, the souvenir shop, where my dad always got me something. Metal detecting on the beach and finding a doll, money and bottle caps, no pirate gold, I think he may have made that up now I'm older LOL. My dad walking along the beach, putting topless limpet shells over his eyes and saying "Ass 'ole Gwasshopper", its a play on words however if you under 40.... (Google David Carradine). When the NEW passports photo-taking machine arrived, the day the Hells Angels came to town, all nice and pleasant during the day, only to break in and trash the place that night.

Swimming in the pool, rides on the train, nudist spying (in later years of course!) chasing rabbits, jumping off the rock (again in later life of course), watching some poor posing man walk up the beach, after water skiing in trunks...what's memorable about that? I hear you ask, all I am going to say is loose legged trunks, plenty of forced water in the nether regions leads to posing man running up the beach with umm how can I say this nicely? LOOSE bowels... it works like an enema!!! Oh how we laughed, he wasn't posing for too long, as he made a speedy exit from the beach! With it being school summer holiday time, the beach was packed! I wonder if he is reading this now and thinking.... "cowbag" (amongst other names, un printable).

The firework displays which always had the biggest pile of wood I had ever seen, although I worried about the hedgehogs and rabbits that might be living in there.... sod the fireworks, I was a

child ALRIGHT!
Radio One Roadshow's seeing: Mike Smith, Steve Wright, Mike Reed, DLT, Gary Davies and more. This was before the MTV Channel was even thought about, and they were the next best thing to actual pop stars!! It's an age thing I think!"

Tami Cross-Halls
(St Austell, Cornwall - Aged 43 and 3/4)

"Emmylou Harris was another favourite who had a young Albert Lee playing in her band.
As I walked into the arena I met a workmate John, his wife and young daughters, he was surprised to see me at the concert – he didn't think C&W was my music!
I said to him "I've come to see Albert Lee play, I've got a cassette by him".
John said to me "he's a family friend and he's coming back to our house tomorrow afternoon to see us".
So I arranged with John to drop the cassette and some Emmylou Harris LP's, which he was playing on, to autograph.
Two to three years ago Albert Lee was playing down in Penzance and I wrote to him to try and find out where John was now, after we lost contact fifteen to twenty years ago.
He said that he thought he was in Derbyshire, but to cut a long story short, Albert Lee is with John's wife now."

K.N. Nankivell (Bodmin, Cornwall)

"I am the only person, who had written permission to use our metal detector on this private beach following being asked to leave Crinnis Beach by a member of staff in 1978 one summer evening with my father & our metal detector (!!) We then wrote to Graham McNally & asked ever so nicely why we couldn't use our metal detector on the beach during the summer evenings looking for 'interesting things'!
We received a very nice letter in response giving us permission for my father & I to use our metal detector on Carlyon Bay Beach (Crinnis Beach).
We found several hundred pounds each summer there consisting mainly of holidaymaker's lost coins as they shook their clothes out & the coins consequently fell into the sand awaiting our discovery each evening!
We even found a nasty looking flicknife one evening, which my father carefully disposed of for safety reasons!!

What great days and evenings they were all those years ago!"
Lee Slaughter (Par, Cornwall)

1979

This year began with the fall of the Pol Pot regime and the Khymer Rouge in Cambodia and the Ayatollah Khomeini returned to seize power in Iran. In San Diego Brenda Ann Spencer killed 2 faculty members and wounded 8 students and a police officer, when she was asked why she did it she said 'I Don't Like Mondays' which went on to inspire the Boomtown Rats to write the song of the same name. Nazi war criminal Josef Mengele died whilst swimming in Brazil, Airey Neave -Conservative MP - was killed in a car bomb attack in the House of Commons car park.

The Dukes of Hazard began on TV, McDonalds introduced the 'Happy Meal', a nudist beach was opened in Brighton and Michael Jackson released his album 'Off The Wall' which sold 7 million copies in America and more worldwide making it an incredibly popular release.

At a different end of the spectrum Mother Theresa won the Nobel Peace prize and Lord Mountbatten was assassinated plus Margaret Thatcher became the first female Prime Minister and Vice President Saddam Hussein became the President of Iraq, but to even up world peace President Sadat of Egypt signed a 'peace treaty' with Prime Minister Menachem Begin of Israel.

In the world of entertainment Sid Vicious died at the age of 21 of a heroin overdose in New York, 'Star Trek the Motion Picture' premiered and Milk And Honey from Israel won Eurovision with 'Hallejuah'.

Celebrity deaths included Joyce Grenfell, Gracie Fields, John Wayne and 'Carry On' films stalwart Peter Butterworth. Jennifer Love Hewitt was born, as well as – James McAvoy, Kate Hudson, Chris Pratt, Kevin Hart and Pete Wentz from Fall Out Boy.

The Christmas number one was an odd, but excellent choice, by the prog rock legends Pink Floyd with 'Another Brick in the Wall (Pt 2)' from their classic album 'The Wall' and the biggest selling single of the year was 'Bright Eyes' by Art Garfunkel from the cartoon film 'Watership Down'.

"In 1979, in the run up to the summer season, Alison McNally mentioned that they were planning to start a roller disco in the main hall. I was a reasonable skater at the time, and spent a lot of time pestering her to let me become one of the roller disco staff. I guess it paid off. Looking after the roller-skating became my main job, for the next few years.

Just before the launch of the roller disco, the McNally's had arranged a feature on BBC's Spotlight, to help promote the opening. Yours truly featured in the small clip that was made in the studio; the track we skated to was Bill Lovelady's 'Reggae For It Now'.

That was it. I was now a regular member of the skating staff, progressing to being the one responsible for collecting the floats for the cash desk and skate hire, making sure the fire exits were all unlocked, and that everything was in place ready to open to the public.

During the summer months, the roller-skating was normally open in the afternoons Monday to Friday, and where possible (depending upon any events that were taking place in the main hall) Saturday mornings, and Sunday afternoons. As well as Tuesday, Friday and Sunday evenings.

It was, by any stretch of the imagination, possibly one of the most enjoyable jobs I've ever had. I spent most of my time honing my skating skills, whilst keeping an eye on the punters, and making sure they kept out of trouble.

As well as the skating, over the next few years, I also did a number of other jobs. In fact, outside of maintenance, lifeguard and catering, I pretty much did most jobs going."

Martyn (aka Skippy) Feather (Lancing, Sussex)

"My first visit, after moving to Plymouth, was in May 1979 when I *went to see Glen Campbell. I was celebrating my 21st and my good friend Ann Pope treated me! His support act was Diane Solomon, an American singer, who was quite popular at the time!"*

Diane Clancy (Plymouth, Devon)

"The roller disco was also a place I frequented as they use to play "I Was Made For Loving You" by Kiss which was also released around 1979!!"

Steve Wade (St Austell, Cornwall)

"Tony Blackburn - People jeered, and mocked his performance. Until he said, "You think I am an idiot, don't you?" The crowd shouted, "YES!" To which he replied "But I didn't come here and pay to see you!"

Clive Rodell (Sydney, Australia)

"I have fond memories of the Coliseum as most of my youth was spent there and my love of music came from the many live gigs I went to there over the years. I think I had the best years of it; my first gig was Stiff Little Fingers in 1979, at the age of 14. My mates and I would go down there most weekends, it was only a few quid a ticket so we would go and see whoever was playing."

Mike Bennett (Cornwall)

"Once the Coliseum was established, I could be found carrying out various tasks, from House Crew, helping bands road crews to bring in and take out their gear. Follow-spot operator, operating one of the two in-house 'Super Troupers'. Usher, bar staff, and occasionally security.

Other jobs were preparing the seating for seated concerts, car park attendant, crazy golf, selling ice creams and souvenirs in the beach shop. In fact, one summer, in the beach shop, just when Sky Lab was due to crash back to earth, I put up a card advertising "Anti-Sky Lab Cream" just for a laugh.

Whilst working at the Coliseum, I saw many acts and bands, as well as being the front part of the reindeer that pulled Jethro on his sleigh, during one of the Christmas shows."

Martyn (aka Skippy) Feather (Lancing, Sussex)

"The first band I saw down there was Slade, in 1979 I think, supported by a punk band called The Drill, who were pretty crap but the lead singer simulated oral sex on the bass player.... weird

how   I   remember   this!!
Other bands include Def Leppard, Iron Maiden, Saxon, Samson (featuring Bruce Dickinson when he was called Bruce Bruce!) on their very early tours. Saw Magnum several times as a support band and then headlining themselves. Motorhead, Sammy Hagar, Alice Cooper, The Scorpions, Kiss (my heroes), Whitesnake, Black Sabbath, Rainbow, Hawkwind, Mike Oldfield, all followed and some damn good support bands including Vardis, Limelight, Waysted, Lita Ford and Wolfsbane to mention just a few!"
Steve Wade (St Austell, Cornwall)

"The amusement arcade was amazing. First 'talking' pinball machine 'Gorgar'. With traditional "new " video games, in the bar (Space Invaders, Kong) in a glass topped table. A TABLE !"
Denis Bennett (St Austell, Cornwall)

"I went to the disco there in the late 70's when it was called Beelzebub (a Devil of a disco!!).
I had to lie about my age to get in, couldn't work out the year

quickly enough and subtracted years instead of adding them. The doorman said 'so that would make you 12 then?

But he let me in anyway! Shortly afterwards it had a refit and became 'Bentleys' the story I heard was that they had to call it something like that as they'd just had a load of carpet made featuring a large letter 'B' possibly apocryphal but it made me laugh at the time!"

Alan Westaway (St Blazey, Cornwall)

"I almost forgot the crazy golf, we used to miss the last hole as the ball would travel down a pipe never to be seen again, so we got our money's worth by having two or three rounds before the final hole and returning the clubs to the kiosk."

Richard Ruse (St Austell, Cornwall)

1980

*P*ierre Trudeau was re-elected in Canada and Robert Mugabe was elected in Zimbabwe, the USA boycotted the summer Olympics in Moscow, there were riots in St Paul's in Bristol and the UK and Spain agreed to re-open the border between Spain and Gibraltar which had been closed since 1969. In the lively world of entertainment Pac Man was released for the first time in Japan, CNN (the Cable News Network) was launched, 'The Empire Strikes Back' was released in cinemas, AC/DC released their classic album 'Back In Black' and Ian Curtis – lead singer of Joy Division was found hanged.

In the UK Ford started producing the Escort Mk3 and British Leyland launched the Metro.

The music world lost three legends this year when John Lennon was shot dead outside the entrance to the Dakota building in New York, John Bonham - drummer with Led Zeppelin - died in his sleep after drinking 40 vodka shots and Bon Scott – lead singer of AC/DC – died in his sleep, choking to death on his own vomit in a Renault 5 outside a house in East Dulwich, London.

Other celebrities who passed away this year included Jimmy Durante, Alfred Hitchcock, runner Jesse Owens, Peter Sellers, Steve McQueen, Mae West and the legend that was Colonel Sanders, the owner and figurehead of KFC (which was still then known as Kentucky Fried Chicken) died of acute leukemia.

Channing Tatum, Steven Gerrard, Venus Williams, Macaulay Culkin, Ryan Gosling, Christina Aguilera and Jake Gyllenhaal were all born this year as well, making the world of movies and sport a much livelier place in years to come.

The biggest selling single of the year title went to 'Don't Stand So Close To Me' The Police and the Christmas number one was a 'one hit wonder' by St Winifreds School Choir with the Christmas classic 'There's No One Quite Like Grandma'.

"First date of the ill-fated 'More Specials Tour' in 1980.
I snuck five people into my hotel room for the night, got caught in the morning and had to pay extra. Grrr!
Good gig though"
Horace Panter (The Specials - Bass)

"MCA secured the support slot for us on Saxon's, 'Wheels of Steel Tour,' in early 1980.
The tour was in two, three-week parts. I think Girlschool did the first three weeks, (we were already out on tour opening up for the Scorpions,) and the Tygers did the second half of the tour. As part of the 'Wheels' tour we had a show on May 26th at the Cornwall Coliseum.

Our two loyal road crew travelled together in our 3-ton truck with our backline and the band, Jess, Rocky, Brian and me, Robb, travelled in our hired Mk II Ford Cortina estate car! I used to do most of the driving and Rocky would read the map and give directions! No sat nav in those days!

We seemed to be driving forever to this mystical place. Down this narrow road, down quite a steep hill and all of a sudden there it was before us.... the Coliseum!

It looked very grand indeed. I remember it was a sunny day and as we drove towards it a wave of excitement came over us all. We pulled up next to Saxon's two trucks, where roadies were working busily away loading in the whole show. Lights, Sound system, Marshall 4x12's, drum riser and kit, front of house mixing console and so much more.

Walking into the place it felt huge, well it was huge, I think it held three and a half thousand at a push and tonight was nearly sold out. When Saxon had finished there sound check it was Tygers time!

Our crew set up our backline, we sound checked and then we were called into Saxon's production office! In there was Biff and their tour manager JJ. Apparently it had been noted that when we were sound checking Rocky and I had walked in front of the monitor line. We were told that when we played we were NOT to do this as Saxon did this in THEIR show! We felt like naughty little boys!

Show time and as soon as our intro tape finished the lights went up and Rocky and I ran straight in front of the monitor line to perform our opening song! Oops!"

Robb Weir (Tygers of Pan Tang – Guitar)

"Did I play there? I'm stumped!
We didn't do a great deal of work in Cornwall; we did play a gig there with the Mechanics. I don't remember a great deal about the gig except that we didn't have a particularly good sound as I recall. My memories aren't too glowing."
Steve Gibbons (Steve Gibbons Band – Vocals / Guitar)

"I used to drive coaches for Wallace Arnold and the first job they gave me after passing my test was to drive some young people to a rock concert which I was delighted to do and at time, in the 80's, you would drive the coach down that very steep hill and park in the car park at the bottom.
When the young people came out of the concert they all got on the coach to return home but the only problem was the coach would not go up the hill with them on board so after several attempts I had to get passengers off the coach and drive up empty and the reload them at the top of the hill; good job they were youngsters and they thought it was good fun, if they were old passengers they would still be there."
Peter Lucas (Plymouth, Devon)

100 Big Names in the Big Hall

NEW CORNISH
RIVIERA LIDO

SAFFRON RECORDS ST. AUSTELL & TRURO ● SOUND MACHINE - NEWQUAY ●

SATURDAY 19TH APRIL POSTPONED TO JUNE 14

MADNESS

Tickets £3.00 In Advance

SATURDAY 26TH APRIL

THE STEVE GIBBONS BAND

Plus the official tour support

your very own MECHANICS

Tickets £2.50 In Advance

DOORS OPEN 8.00 p.m.

COMING SOON

IAN DURY & THE BLOCKHEADS   THE CLASH   IRON MAIDEN   CHUCK BERRY   THE PHOTOS   THE JAM

NEW CORNISH RIVIERA LIDO
CARLYON BAY, ST. AUSTELL. TEL. PAR 4261

TICKETS AVAILABLE FROM VIRGIN RECORDS - PLYMOUTH

MR. PICKWICK - CAMBORNE ● JAMES MUSIC - PENZANCE ●

"My all time favourite Coliseum experience was at The Specials, must have been 1980'ish? An amazing gig where a sizeable contingent of the mosh pit (including me) managed to clamber on the stage.

Terry and the band then stopped the bouncers from turfing us off and we stayed on stage for a song before leaping off into the crowd.

Great music and a fantastic positive vibe... Ska rules!!!

Mark Bishop (Christchurch, New Zealand)

"The Nolans was my first concert there, in 1980, 8 years old fully seated.
I went to the toilet during the concert and they were giving kids lolly pops from the stage out of seaside buckets, I was so chuffed I got a lolly."

Julie Smith (Plymouth, Devon)

"Oh, my..........The Samson gig was organised by Mid Cornwall College of Further Education Students Union as an alternative to our usual (very successful) college dances. I was on the committee who organised it and it wasn't as well supported as we had hoped.............I started smoking that night.
No wonder we made no money on that gig. I think we had to hand over all the Student Union reserves to pay the band. I took to the Little Girls Room to hide when I heard that a couple of the lads had been summonsed by the band's manager to pay them and I knew we didn't have enough money to pay them."

Sarah Newton (Cornwall)

"I remember the Samson gig. I only found out about it when I saw

a poster in Saffron Records in St Austell a few days before.
My mate Martin Collings and I went. I think it cost us £2 a ticket, which was really cheap in those days. It was a shame that there were only about 100 people in the Coliseum that night. Samson weren't the biggest name band, but they were great live and it was a great gig.
They had a brilliant drummer called Thunderstick who wore a mask and had his drum kit set up in a cage. The lead vocalist wasn't bad either - some bloke called Bruce Bruce. Soon after, he left Samson and joined an up and coming band called Iron Maiden and became known by his real name of Bruce Dickinson!
Wonder what happened to them?!"

Jon Simmons (St Austell)

"Saw the Specials there, excellent act.
A fight broke out during their set and the lead singer stopped singing and called for the lights to go up and then shouted at the scrappers until they stopped and left; then they played again!"

Jim Rolfe (St Tudy, Cornwall)

"I remember myself and a dozen other Mods and Skinheads scrambling our way onto the Coliseum stage at The Specials concert, Terry Hall the lead singer sang, and we danced as if our lives depended on it!!! When the song finish Terry thanked us all and the bouncers carefully helped us down from the stage.
What the bouncers should have done was give us all a clip round the ear hole and a good talking to for getting up there, but they seemed to know how important the bands were to us in our younger years. Top Guys!!!"

Alison Hall (Par, Cornwall)

BeetleBug
NEW CORNISH
RIVIERA LIDO

WED 2nd JULY 1980 — 8.00 p.m.

MCCFE Students Union

Presents
Samson

PLUS
SUPPORT

TICKETS
£2.00

TICKETS AVAILABLE FROM:— ROBBIES RECORDS – NEWQUAY
SAFFRON RECORDS – ST. AUSTELL & TRURO JAMES MUSIC – PENZANCE
VIRGIN RECORDS – PLYMOUTH MR. PICKWICK – CAMBORNE

NEW CORNISH RIVIERA LIDO
CARLYON BAY, ST. AUSTELL TEL. PAR 4281

"I started work at the Coliseum in November 1980 it was one of the last concerts that we built the raked seating from scratch. It was stored in a number of old lorry bodies and comprised of the steelwork flooring and seating it took a team of something like 15 men all day to build it. After that I continued to work on the get in and get outs in the hall. This involved very long days starting very early in the morning and not finishing until very late at night. During my time there I worked in a number of jobs. As well as the work I did in the hall I also did the following jobs:- Usher (Male Usherette), Bar staff, Amusement Arcade Attendant, Roller skate issue, Beach Attendant and Lifeguard." **Andy**

Gill (Coliseum Staff, St Austell, Cornwall)

"My dad took me to see Roy Orbison, we were quite near the front row I must've been about 6 years old. I still remember it and his amazing voice. Completely overwhelmed, great father and daughter bonding.
Like many people who went to Gossips I got asked out and am married to the most amazing man 13 years on and have two beautiful children.

Happy memories."
Sophie Kitts (Tywardreath, Cornwall)

Saxon @ Cornwall Coliseum
20th November 1980

Heavy Metal Thunder

Hungry Years

See the Light Shining

20,000ft

Judgement Day

Taking Your Chances

Freeway Mad

Sixth Form Girls

Rainbow Theme

Frozen Rainbow

Stand Up and Be Counted

Dallas 1pm

To Hell and Back Again

Strong Arm of the Law

747 (Strangers in the Night)

Wheels of Steel
Machine Gun

"After being released from France having been jailed for inciting a riot. I remember being wedged between a mass of bodies only moving to and fro with the surging crowd.
The band played songs from their 'Raven' album as well as their other top recordings. The band were menacing with Burnel's bass.
I remember a large lady had fainted and the stage staff couldn't lift her onto the stage but finally managed it. It was so hot!!
Met the band afterwards and got autographs. A brill night for me."
Gary Warne (St Austell)

"The gig which had the biggest impact on me was the Stranglers first gig there in July 1980. I was a big fan before they came, so was hugely excited when it was announced. Then doubt was cast as to whether it would happen, as the band was imprisoned in Nice for starting a riot! Thankfully they were released in time. First song was 'Shah Shah a-go-go', and the sight of JJ Burnel prowling the stage with his black Fender Precision left a lasting impression. Other songs I remember are 'Duchess', 'Nuclear Device', 'Tank' (a particular favourite) and the big hits like 'No More Heroes' and 'Peaches'. I saw them every time they played there and many *times since.*

I am still a Stranglers fan, but that first Coliseum gig is the one that started it all. I was inspired to play the bass after seeing JJ Burnel of the Stranglers in July 1980 (and every other time they played there) and I still play it now (with the Steely-eyed Missile Men-a Shuker   JJ   Burnel   bass!)."

Mike Bennett (Cornwall)

"I was interviewed for a job as an usherette by Mike Honeyman in the early 1980's and joined the team. Sometimes we would work once a week and others four nights a week.

I met a young man there called Andy and one thing lead to another and one night in the Ocean Suite he got down on one knee and asked me to marry him. We got married on 2nd April 1983 with Mike (who only had sons) giving me away and his son David (who was also an usher) being best man.

We had our evening party at the Ocean Suite for friends and family the other ushers and usherettes attending after the Leo Sayer gig in the hall.

Another couple who worked at Cornwall Coliseum Keith Menear and Denise Hawken got married on the same day and Denise and I got into trouble with Sandie Gregory because we couldn't work for the show. I hasten to add we are both still married and exchange cards on our wedding anniversary."

Sheila Gill (Usherette – St Austell, Cornwall)

Iron Maiden @ Cornwall Coliseum
30th May 1980

Sanctuary
Wrathchild
Prowler
Remember Tomorrow
Killers
Running Free
Another Life

Transylvania
Strange World
Charlotte the Harlot
Phantom of the Opera
Iron Maiden
Drifter
I Got the Fire

**Mike Oldfield @ Cornwall Coliseum
June 19th 1980**

Platinum, Part 1
Platinum, Part 2
Platinum, Part 3
Platinum, Part 4
I Got Rhythm
Punkadiddle
Incantations (Part 1)
Incantations (Part 2)
Incantations (Part 3)
Incantations (Part 4)
Tubular Bells, Part One
Tubular Bells, Part Two
Guilty
Ommadawn, Part One
Blue Peter
Portsmouth
Polka
Radetsky March
Blaydon Races

1981

*T*he year began with Greece joining the European Union and Ronald Reagan became the new President of the United States and two months later he was shot in the chest in an attempted assassination in Washington D.C.

The first 'London Marathon' was ran with only 7,500 people taking part, Bucks Fizz won Eurovision with 'Making Your Mind Up' tearing off their skirts in the process, the first Coca-Cola bottling plant was opened in China, the 'Prog Rock' band Yes split (getting back together in several versions in years to follow), Bobby Sands of the Provisional IRA died from hunger strike, in the cinema 'Raiders of the Lost Ark' was released, the 'Toxteth Riots' took place in Liverpool, the first game of 'Paintball' was played in New Hampshire, USA and 'Donkey Kong' was released in arcades by games giant Nintendo.

The summer TV schedule was dominated by the highlight that was the 'Royal Wedding of Prince Charles to Lady Diana Spencer at St Paul's Cathedral in London. The event was watched by over 700 million people on television worldwide.

Mark Chapman was sentenced to 20 years to life in prison for the killing of John Lennon the previous year, the very first episode of the classic TV comedy 'Only Fools and Horses' was broadcast on the BBC, Simon & Garfunkel performed their concert in Central Park to over 500,000 people and the event was later released as a video and album, the Police had one of the biggest albums of the year with 'Ghost in the Machine', Anwar Sadat – the Egyptian President was assassinated at a military parade and 'Penlee Lifeboat Distaster' occured off the coast of Cornwall with the loss of sixteen people, including eight voluntary lifeboatmen.

The world of music lost Bill Haley and the world of cinema

lost Natalie Wood, William Holden, Bernard Lee – who played 'M' in the James Bond films and Lotte Lenya who played Bond's main adversary Rosa Klebb in the film 'From Russia With Love.' Actor Elijah Wood was born this year, in addition to Alicia Keys, Roger Federer, Justin Timberlake, Tom Hiddleston, Paris Hilton, Beyoncé, Josh Groban, Natalie Portman, Britney Spears, Chris Evans and Brandon Flowers – lead singer of The Killers.

The Christmas Number One and the best selling single of the year were the same this year with 'Don't You Want Me?' by the Human League – the main forerunners of the 'New Romantic' electronic music revolution that was taking place at the time, which included Depeche Mode, Duran Duran, Spandau Ballet and Soft Cell amongst many.

"I've no real stories to tell about the venue, however this was the first date in what was affectionately termed as the 'shit tour' for a couple of reasons.
The first was that Mick and David were at one another's throats after Mick's girlfriend had moved in with David just days before, and secondly because David didn't like the design of the stage set and the tour was very nearly cancelled the day before it began (or perhaps that was an excuse not to go on tour … who knows).
I kept a journal, and in it, it states that my headphones blew in soundcheck and I had to borrow someone else's and that what remained of the stage design was taken down, leaving only the rostrums. Apparently, what with all that, I thought the show was 'average considering'."
Steve Jansen (Japan – Drums)

Japan @ Cornwall Coliseum
December 7th 1981

Canton
Swing
Gentlemen Take Polaroids
Alien

Talking Drum
Visions Of China
Quiet Life
My New Career
Ghosts
Cantonese Boy
Methods of Dance
Still Life in Mobile Homes
European Son
The Art Of Parties
Life In Tokyo
Fall In Love With Me
Canton

"Apart from my rock and metal, Japan were one of the few other type of bands that I listened to – my tastes have become extremely eclectic since I turned thirty though.

They had recently had two Top 40 singles with 'Quiet Life' and 'Visions Of China', which the tour was named after, so the show was sold out.

The support band were up and coming electronic band Blancmange, a year before they were to hit the Top 40 with their 'Top Ten' hit 'Living On The Ceiling', with Top Of The Pops appearances as well; their support slot on this tour was what broke them and they must have felt indebted to Japan for the vast exposure.

Japan were sublime. Their music was inspiring and this show was one of my favourites so far, having only started going to gigs in 1981 anyway, plus they were so different to any gigs that I had attended so far. They were cool, David Sylvian's vocals were silky smooth and Mick Karn's fretless basswork was astounding, an amazing show from a band just reaching the peak of their popularity."

Ian Carroll (Author, Plymouth)

Black Sabbath @ Cornwall Coliseum
February 2nd 1981

War Pigs
Neon Knights
N.I.B
Lady Evil
Sweet Leaf
Children of the Sea
Black Sabbath
Heaven and Hell

Iron Man
Sabbath Bloody Sabbath
Orchid
Die Young
Paranoid
Children of the Grave

"Sometimes we would also be asked to stage crew for the show and this would involve all sorts of tasks including for Black Sabbath winding the bars in on stage that held a massive cross full of lights and at another Black Sabbath Concert they also used large propane flame throwers along the front of the stage and we were in the pit at the front of the stage and things got more than a little warm." **Andy Gill (Coliseum Staff, St Austell, Cornwall)**

"It was Feb 1981 when as a wide eyed 17 year old I was taken to the Cornwall Coliseum to see my first band live. The band were Black Sabbath with Ronnie James Dio as their vocalist and the first time always lives with you.
The atmosphere, the venue, the cross section of people, it was such a buzz. I remember thinking how loud and fuzzy the sound was but after the gig I was hooked.
The Coliseum then became a godsend for my hunger for more live music and I was lucky enough to live in Plymouth at a time when a lot of bands used the Coliseum as a warm up for their tours of the UK.
As I'm now in my 50's some of the memories are vague and a lot of my ticket stubs which I still collect were lost (thrown out by my father who thought he was 'tidying my room'). I have found three stubs, one of Saxon and two of Roy 'Chubby' Brown!
P.S: I have forgiven my dad."
Theo Christian (Gateshead)

"One of the more occasional jobs I carried out was that of "emergency" DJ. Normally this would be OK, as one of the regular DJs would leave a collection of discs for me to use. However, on one particular night, I was asked to DJ for the after concert disco

for an Ultravox gig.

The only regular DJ on site was booked for the Ocean Suite. We had to arrange for a runner to go between Bentleys and the Ocean Suite, to bring me a few discs, to keep me going. We managed it, but, thanks to the "stress", I was a little worse for wear, alcohol wise, by the end of the evening."

Martyn (aka Skippy) Feather (Lancing, Sussex)

"With the huge success of the 'Wildcat,' album in 1980 and the addition of John Sykes and Jon Deverill to the Tygers line up, MCA wanted a new album. 'Spellbound' was recorded and released and a full British tour was booked to promote the album. On the 25th of April 1981 the Spellbound tour pulled into the car park of the Cornwall Coliseum. Two forty foot articulated lorries, two sixteen-berth 'Nightliners', a ten tonne truck and a stray dog that followed us down the lane! Having played the Coliseum the year before with Saxon we knew what to expect in terms of layout. The building itself was very impressive, although it appeared quite old, you got a very welcoming feeling and once you were inside you felt you were somewhere special.

The layout as I remember it from a performer's point of view was a very large oblong shaped interior, with the stage running down one of the long sides and on the other side of the auditorium a long bar serving all sort of refreshments. The main doors were at one end. We had quite a big show for the time, and I remember our light show looked particularly impressive in there as we could get our lights higher up than in a City Hall giving them a better spread and focus. We had two support bands, Alcatraz and Magnum, who both performed perfectly. The Coliseum was sold out and when it came to Tyger show time the atmosphere in the place was electric. Queue the dry ice, the intro tape and the pyrotechnics! The Coliseum is without doubt one of the nicest venues I have played, such a shame it has gone. Progress...really?"

Robb Weir (Tygers of Pan Tang – Guitar)

Cornwall Coliseum — CARLYON BAY

Charley Pride IN CONCERT with THE PRIDESMEN plus LITTLE GINNY

APRIL

MAY

THE SPINNERS IN CONCERT

"A STAR AMONG STARS"

CORNISH HOT ROCKS !
RADIO ACTIVE
CHAIN REACTION
RISK BUSINESS
LIVE IN A 4 HOUR SHOW

GLEN CAMPBELL with SPECIAL GUEST
DIANE SOLOMON — TANYA TUCKER

CLEO LAINE & The John Dankworth Quintet

CORNWALL INDUSTRIES FAIR 1981
A MAJOR EXHIBITION OF REGIONAL ENTERPRISE, INCLUDING BOATING & OUTDOOR LEISURE FEATURES

THE GREATEST ELECTRIC FOLK BAND
STEELEYE SPAN

BBC TV's
ANTIQUES ROADSHOW
ARTHUR NEGUS & Guest Experts assess your ANTIQUES or NOT-SO-ANTIQUES?

FUN-FILLED FAMILY SHOW
ANIMAL KWACKERS ★ Ideal Bank Holiday Treat for the under 10's ★
THE CHILDREN'S T.V. FAVOURITES

HEAVY METAL TRIPLE!!!
+ MAGNUM
+ ALCATRAZ

LEO SAYER

"I was only 15 years old.
For the last 4 years all I had listened to was rock music and heavy metal. I had an army surplus camouflaged jacket that was covered in patches, Judas Priest on the back across my shoulders and various smaller KISS patches and badges of Black Sabbath, Rainbow and more on the front.
I had badgered my parents to allow me to go to see a 'rock show' at the Cornwall Coliseum and this would be my night, my first ever gig!
I went with one of my best friends at the time, Christopher Boyce; he was just 16 and so just slightly older than me.
We got an organised coach from Plymouth Bretonside bus station and within an hour we were at the Cornwall Coliseum.
Too young to drink alcohol and much to young looking to even think about getting served, we went straight down to the front and watched the first band on – Alcatraz.
The band were a 'run of the mill' rock band, the only thing that stood out was their cover of 'You're The One That I Want' from Grease, which all the audience thought was hilarious.
Second on was the band that myself and my mate had both come to see most – Magnum.

We had both loved the band for the last couple of years and had played to death a live cassette of them at the Reading Festival in 1980, which Christopher had recorded off the 'Friday Rock Show' on Radio One.

They played classic songs such as 'Changes', 'All Of My Life', 'Invasion' and 'Kingdom Of Madness' – we were on 'cloud nine' when they finished, our hair shaken to and fro as we rocked out to one of our favourite bands.

The headliners that night (and still playing today) were the Tygers of Pan Tang and being part of the NWOBHM (New Wave Of British Heavy Metal) they were riding high, I even bought a 'Spellbound' t-shirt, which was their current album and thanks to some spending money from my mum, I was able to get a Magnum t-shirt as well.

Band of the night though were definitely Magnum, who are still selling out shows today and are still a favourite of mine, thirty four years later."

Ian Carroll (Author, Plymouth)

The Clash @ Cornwall Coliseum
October 15th 1981

Broadway
One More Time
Know Your Rights
The Guns of Brixton
Train In Vain
(White Man) In Hammersmith Palais
The Magnificent Seven
Ivan Meets GI Joe
Clash City Rockers
Koka Kola
Junco Partner

The Leader
Bankrobber
Somebody Got Murdered
London Calling
Clampdown
Radio Clash
Ghetto Defendant
Charlie Don't Surf
Stay Free
Brand New Cadillac
Safe European Home
Janie Jones
Armagideon Time
Complete Control
Career Opportunities
London's Burning
I Fought The Law
White Riot

Cornwall Coliseum CARLYON BAY

LATE EXTRA
WEDNESDAY
11th NOVEMBER 8pm
ARENA £4 BALCONY £5

Thin Lizzy
+ SWEET SAVAGE

OCTOBER

STATE '81
The St. Austell Trades
Exhibition
★★★★★ A 5 DAY 5 STAR SHOW ★★★★★
Exhibitions, Demonstrations, Giveaways,
Attractions of ALL KINDS. Something for
ALL THE FAMILY ● Plus 10 Royal Wedding
Rides ● Top T.V. Personalities to meet in
person ● 40 years of Ford competition cars
● Vintage motor cycles ● Craftsmen at work
● Fashion Shows ● Plymouth Sound Radio
● Over 100 Trade Stands
Crowns given away each day ● Helicopter
Family Fun!

ULTRAVOX
IN CONCERT
+ EDDIE & SUNSHINE

TUES
13th
7.30pm
ARENA £4.50
RAISED
STALLS
£4.50

THURS
15th
8pm
ARENA
£3.50

THE **CLASH**
Plus SUPPORT

POSTPONED UNTIL
29th NOVEMBER

GILLAN
+ BUDGIE AND NIGHTWING

THURS 29th
8pm
ARENA
£4

ANDY WILLIAMS
with Orchestra and Singers
plus SPECIAL GUEST
JERRY STEVENS

SAT 31st
6.15pm
£6, £8
8pm
£5, £7

NOVEMBER

Transferred from
previous advertised date
MADNESS
+ BELLE STARS

ARENA £4
BALCONY £4

GENTLEMAN'S
SPORTING EVENING
featuring 12 BOUT —
DINNER/BOXING TOURNAMENT
Cornwall Association of
BOYS CLUBS v ROYAL NAVY
Dress — Dinner Jackets
table combants required when
booking (All table Sizes available)

SUPER CABARET DOUBLE BILL
It's a Cracker!!

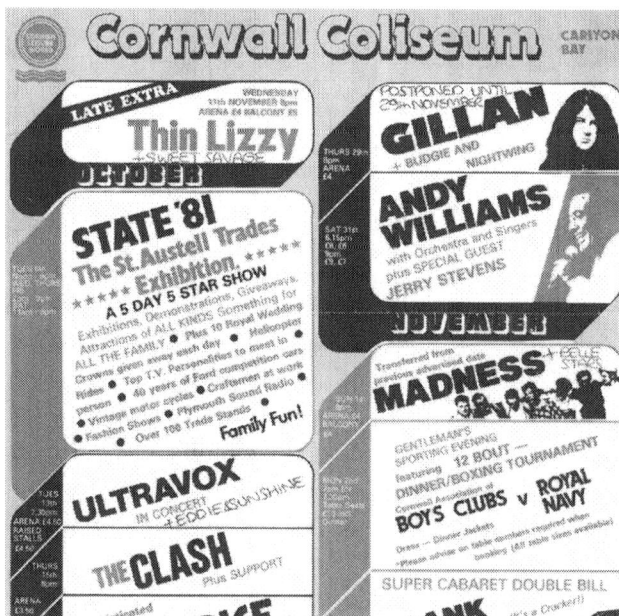

*"Life at the Coliseum in the late 70's and early 80's (my era!!).
Saw some ripping bands from the very first (The Skids swiftly
followed by Stiff Little Fingers) through to some right dross.
The one that sticks in my mind the most is the mighty, awesome,
never to be repeated Clash gig!!!!
The evening started well with a few pints in the Queen's Head and
then I think it was 7 of us piled into my pal's Mini for the short drive
down to the Coliseum. It was already a great night because my
mate H, from Plymouth, who had previously lived in St. Austell had
come back down to his "home patch" and brought some of his
"crowd" down with him. I can't remember all the names but I do
recall John Blowers being one of the guys that came down with H.
I genuinely can't recall who the support band (if any) was but I DO
remember that pre-gig sense of anticipation in the crowd. All the
local "faces" were out in force and we all seemed to sense that it
was going to be a special night. We didn't really realise at the time
that we were somewhat spoilt by having a gig venue locally that
nearly all the big names included on their itinerary. It seemed a
matter of course that we should be able to see The Jam,
Motorhead, The Specials et al just down the road.
I do remember that roar as the band took to the stage and*

wondering to myself just HOW wild it was going to get. Sandinista had been released a few months ago (my Xmas money had been earmarked for the much talked about triple album) and I was also dying to see what the blend was going to be between the "new" stuff and the older stuff from the first album, 'Give 'em Enough Rope' and 'London Calling'. What I wasn't prepared for was the intensity of the pogoing/moshing - and what made it even more surprising was that people were going batshit crazy to "Broadway" ..... "Broadway" ffs, possibly one of the least intense, mellow, laid back offerings the Clash ever recorded!! I can clearly remember thinking what the hell will happen if/when they do "White Riot"!!! Genuinely the most explosive start to a gig I have ever experienced.

Having been such a massive fan for so long it was the culmination to years of waiting for a chance to see "my" band live, and they didn't let me down. Near enough to the front of the crowd to feel that sway and movement of bodies and close enough to Mick (I was standing a little left of centre as you faced the stage) to be entranced by his chops and manic running around the stage. Joe was on fine form, chatting to us between songs and Paul looked as cool as ever. It's difficult to explain but it seemed like a sorta "family" atmosphere - a realisation that we were all just a little bit pissed off with the politics and mainstream culture of the early Thatcher years BUT we could all scream and shout and lose ourselves in some sort of loud, high energy, post-punk celebration of being alive. Plus there was none of the stupid "hero worship" that you got sometimes with other bands - Joe, Mick, Paul and Topper were like your slightly older mates who happened to be in a band AND made you feel that you could be up there with them. In fact several guys from the crowd did just that - I forget the song but one of the local punks (with a VERY impressive Mohican) shared a mic with Paul and there was NO question of him being kicked off the stage.

An awesome set that seemed to flash by and, of course, I got to find out how wild we would all get when "White Riot" DID put in an appearance!!"

Steve Ford (Cornwall)

"Seeing the worst band of my life, the AK Band (I think) who supported The Kinks."

Theo Christian (Gateshead)

"Not a long story but me and my friend went to see Adam And The Ants. About half way through the concert Adam tripped over the light box on the stage.
He fell flat on his face and hurt his knee but like a trooper he carried on till the end limping all the way."
Sean Barbery (St Austell, Cornwall)

"Another great memory & claim to fame involved Girlschool & their support band (I believe the support band was A II Z).
I went to the gig (must have been around the end of 1980 'ish) & was having a post gig party.
I met the bands after the show and cheekily asked them if they fancied going back to mine to party! They accepted and I got to have a smoochie dance with Kim McAuliffe! And very nice it was!!"
Paul Marsh (Cornwall)

"We had our own room on the left hand of the auditorium were we met before the gigs to find out where we were working and to find out any special jobs for the night.
One night some security people came in and asked us to leave because their performer wanted to come into the hall. We were all very surprised considering the stars we had worked for and were not sure what Shakin' Stevens thought we were going to do to him."
Sheila Gill (Usherette – St Austell, Cornwall)

"Growing up in Plymouth In the 80's, the largest venue for a concert in Devon or Cornwall was the Cornwall Coliseum.
My first concert at the age of 15 was at the Coliseum and it was Thin Lizzy in the summer of '81, on their 'Chinatown' tour (£4 concert ticket!).
Phil Lynott playing the classics on his mirrored pick guard bass guitar, shining around the venue. "What an introduction to rock concerts".
I can remember that tickets for the Coliseum could be purchased from Virgin Records, Rivals Records or HMV. Coach tickets to the venue were about a pound and Bretonside Bus/Coach station would be lined up with denim and leather fans, ready to embark on to 4 or 5 coaches for the evening's entertainment."
Mark Jewitt (Plymouth, Devon)

"Shakin' Stevens, the sexiest Welshman in Denim who wrote the

song for me- 'Oh Julie" (If you love me truly-1981).
I was so lucky I was bought a black satin Shakin' Stevens scarf
with fringing which had a gold picture of Shaky' on it, I was also
bought a white Shakin' Stevens pillowcase, as a 7yr old I would
sleep with my face next to his!!
30yrs later and still with my pillowcase I went to see him again on
his 30yr Anniversary tour in Fowey. I stayed behind like a groupie
and he signed my 30yr old pillowcase!!"

Julie Smith (Plymouth, Devon)

"Other memories include being lifted off my feet when waiting for
Whitesnake to come on as the crowd pushed towards the stage. A
little bit scary.
Going to the incredibly long bar for drinks when the drum solos
were on (not a fan)."

Theo Christian (Gateshead)

"The Nolan's did a summer season and the usherettes learnt their
dance routines and I can remember us and some of the audience
watching them performing the routine at the top of the raked
seating. They did a brilliant job."

Sheila Gill (Usherette – St Austell, Cornwall)

Thin Lizzy @ Cornwall Coliseum
August 2nd 1981

Are You Ready?
Genocide (The Killing of the Buffalo)
Waiting For An Alibi
Jailbreak
Killer On The Loose
Trouble Boys
Don't Believe A Word
Memory Pain
Got To Give It Up
Chinatown
Hollywood (Down On Your Luck)
Cowboy Song
The Boys Are Back In Town
Suicide
Roisin Dubh (Black Rose)
Sugar Blues
Baby Drives Me Crazy
Angel Of Death
Rosalie

"The first time that I saw Thin Lizzy was on the 'Renegade' tour and I was still pretty much in my 'gig infancy' having only gone to shows since April of this year.
This was also the last tour to feature Snowy White who went in to regularly play as Roger Waters 'live' guitarist in his band.

The show was amazing, was else would it be? And Phil Lynott dragged the most out of the crowd as he always did."
Ian Carroll (Author, Plymouth)

"Getting the chance to see Thin Lizzy there three times.
What a fantastic live show with a phenomenal front man in Phil Lynott.
So, I have a lot to thank The Coliseum for when it comes to live music, because without it I probably wouldn't be so addicted as I am now.
Theo Christian (Gateshead)

"I recall my first gig was Thin Lizzy in 1981 (birthday present) and, with my customary post autographs wait I ended up chatting to the bouncers afterwards while I was waiting for Dad - in jeans, long greasy rocker hair and too tight t-shirts for a man.
It was funny to see them just two weeks later doing a much more genteel version of bouncing at the Elkie Brooks gig (also a birthday present) wearing penguin suits (set off nicely with long greasy rocker hair).
Mind you, that Elkie Brooks gig was a rocking one!"
Trevor Raggatt (London)

"Ginger Baker - I had to deliver a message to the guitar player in the band that was deemed 'important'.
There were 'cabins' out the back for the artists. I knocked on the door and someone said, "come in" (not Ginger). I had only just opened the door and Ginger looked up and before I had uttered anything said "close the door when you leave!"
Not one for adhering to rude requests, I responded "I will when I have delivered this message. The guitarist took the written message and was extremely courteous in thanking me.... much to Bakers annoyance. I then said "I'll close the door when I leave"
Clive Rodell (Sydney, Australia)

Glen Campbell @ Cornwall Coliseum
8th May 1981

Rhinestone Cowboy
Gentle on My Mind

Wichita Linesman
Galveston
Country Boy (You Got Your Feet
in L.A.)
By the Time I Get to Phoenix
Dreams of the Everyday Housewife
Heartache Number Three
Please Come to Boston
Trials and Tribulations
It's Only Make Believe
Crying
Foggy Mountain Breakdown/ Orange
Blossom Special
Milk Cow Blues
Roll in My Sweet Baby's Arms
I'm So Lonesome I Could Cry
Southern Nights
Amazing Grace
Try a Little Kindness
Loving Arms
It's Your World Boys and Girls
Mull of Kintyre

"The Adam and the Ants concert, all evening young ladies were being carried out and taken to another room because they swooned. They returned when feeling better only to be cross because they had lost their front positions."

Sheila Gill (Usherette – St Austell, Cornwall)

"One of the best value and enjoyable concerts was Adam and the Ants. Really long sets with the interval showing all his recent OTT videos on a huge screen."

Denis Bennett (St Austell, Cornwall)

"Adam and the Ants, played they stayed at Fowey Hotel.
We the 'fans' went down to Fowey after school, waited outside the hotel, and these guys emerged from the hotel, we asked them if they had seen Adam and the Ants, they said 'no', anyway, we were only asking the 'Ants', if they had seen 'Adam and the ants', only they were not wearing their make-up and costumes, and we didn't recognise them!!! Some fans eh??
I did get a picture of me with Adam, but I cut myself out of it because I had a god awful hairstyle!!!"

Nancy (St Blazey, Cornwall)

"My favourite ever show was Adam and the Ants, 'The Prince Charming Review'. It was a fantastic show and the girl's screams were deafening!"

Gary Cocks (Falmouth, Cornwall)

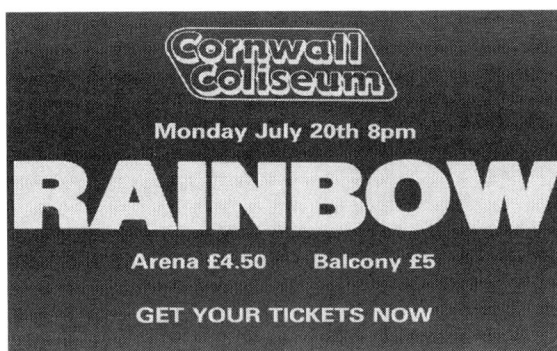

"At the time, Richie Blackmore's band Rainbow was incredibly popular. Having been one of the mainstays in Deep Purple, he and Roger Glover had gone on to form Rainbow, now in their 3rd incarnation having lost both Ronnie James Dio (RIP) and Graham Bonnet to other projects - Dio was now fronting Black Sabbath and Bonnet was with MSG the Michael Schenker Group.
New lead singer Joe Lynn Turner was proving very popular with

the ladies and the hits kept coming - this tour was the 'Difficult To Cure' tour and was straight off the back of a popular album and a hit single in 'I Surrender'.

The support was the brilliantly aggressive Aussie's 'Rose Tattoo' - years before Angry Anderson sang Scott & Charlene's wedding song on Neighbours 'Suddenly' and 27 years before I interviewed him with my son at Download Festival 2008."

Ian Carroll (Author, Plymouth)

"Angry Anderson of Rose Tattoo cutting his head open after head-butting a speaker."

Theo Christian (Gateshead)

"The thing I remember most about the gig, apart from the fact that Ian Gillan is an awesome front man, is meeting him after the gig. We chatted briefly and I got his autograph! As I left he shook my hand and said "Stay cool,man!"

Paul Marsh (Cornwall)

The Who @ Cornwall Coliseum
January 31st 1981

Substitute
I Can't Explain
Baba O'Riley
The Quiet One
Don't Let Go The Coat
Sister Disco
Music Must Change
You Better You Bet Drowned
Another Tricky Day
Behind Blue Eyes
Pinball Wizard

My Generation
What'cha Gonna Do About It
Won't Get Fooled Again
5:15
Long Live Rock
Who Are You?
Let's See Action
Bargain
The Punk and the Godfather
The Real Me
Naked Eye
Love, Reign O'er Me
Twist and Shout

"I never worked at the Coliseum but worked in a shop called 'M K Morris Newsagent' which was on Beach Road; it was the last shop before the Coliseum.

I was 17 when The Who were headlining on 30th and 31st January 1981. Tickets were to go on sale on a Sunday morning and I watched from the shop as streams of cars passed, full of lucky occupants going to buy their tickets.

I finished work at 12:30 but was then under 'house arrest' until lunch was over. I don't think I was released until nearly 15:00 and I was convinced that all the tickets would be sold; rumours had reached the shop of queues round the car park.

Eventually I got to the Box Office above the Wimpy and couldn't believe that there were only a couple of people ahead of me. More surprisingly, there were tickets left!

Clutching my chequebook – an obsolete method of payment peculiar to the 20th Century – I managed to purchase the tickets. I was armed with a shopping list from college and I seem to remember my total purchase being £32.

I enjoyed the night – I went on the Saturday. There was sufficient

space to move around comfortably but enough of a crowd to necessitate 'stilts'. Being a bit little, I couldn't see so gathered a number of plastic glasses. Having made 2 equally sized piles, I tipped them over on the floor and climbed aboard – instant visual of the stage!
Happy days."
Sarah Newton (Cornwall)

"Aaah the Coliseum.... memories, driving down from Plymouth after the clubs kicked out one Saturday night to get tickets for the Who..... And smoking a bit to much on the way to the actual gig, getting out the car and that is all I remember.... apparently I was having a great time, just don't remember it..."
Chris Martin-Gathern (Dikanäs, Västerbottens Län, Sweden)

"I have a lot of memories of the Coliseum having played down there several times. But the one that stays in my memory above all others is the day we were in the arcade as we always were in the early 80's.
We were Teddy boys and as it was getting toward dusk a few guys came up to us and said, "you know who are playing here tonight?" We said "no" They said "the Who." We said "so what" They said "there are about 100 Lambettas down there and 200 mods."
The ten of us ran out of the arcade and up the cliffs chased by hundreds of mods. They followed us over the golf course and we managed to hide up the trees in Cyprus Avenue woods. We could hear them below us. We were very quiet. Good times."
Chris Budge (St Austell, Cornwall)

"I think The Who were the first band to play there after they lowered the ceiling for a better sound"
K.N. Nankivell (Bodmin, Cornwall)

"Crikey the many events I went to at this place I don't have enough fingers and toes for to count with.
Celebrations galore. My aunt had her wedding reception there and the photos I remember had the palm trees behind.
I have so many happy memories. Roller disco and night clubs with all the name changes over the years. For me as I teenager at 14 I loved this place as there was nothing else like it.
Many a concert I saw and too many to mention.

Also the 'Roadshows'.
Spent all my youth and older years there.
Sitting in the Wimpy and the arcade. The place was buzzing once upon a time and it was the best in the west.
Got in free few times as knew bouncers on door. Whoops!"
Sharon Stoneman (St Austell, Cornwall)

"One of my least enjoyed gigs was Elvis Costello. If memory serves, he came on, played his 'yet unreleased' stuff & none of his recent hits."
Denis Bennett (St Austell, Cornwall)

"I saw Elvis Costello and the Attractions there, great gig, but the 'punk' audience spent most of the show spitting at Elvis, poor fella had it running down his face, but he didn't seem to care, in fact, I'm sure he was spitting back!"
Alan Westaway (St Blazey, Cornwall)

"I have memories of the custom car show that was held in the main hall and the 'State 81' exhibition, as my uncle had a stand selling tools, so I spent most of the day looking at all that Cornwall had to offer."
Richard Ruse (St Austell, Cornwall)

"I saw Adam and the Ants at the Cornwall Coliseum, it was certainly sometime of the year, it was a sunny day I remember that clearly. I went with some acquaintance and her father drove us down in his car, because at the time I didn't have a driving licence or a car, I just had a motorbike.
I had make-up, it wasn't my make-up I have to say, I borrowed

some of hers - it did look lovely.
I had the stripe across my nose - I was an 'Adam' and I went there
with this person that I knew and then we saw him and it was good
and it was when he dressed up as 'Prince Charming', I almost
cried it was really emotional."
Mike Horton (Plymouth, Devon)

Elvis Costello & The Attractions
@ Cornwall Coliseum
March 1st 1981

Accidents Will Happen
The Beat
Possession
Strict Time
Luxembourg
Clowntime Is Over
Watch Your Step
I've Been Born Again / King Horse
Human Hands
Secondary Modern
Big Sisters' Clothes
From a Whisper to a Scream
Watching the Detectives / Master -
Blaster
I Can't Stand Up for Falling Down
Pump It Up

Cornwall Coliseum
CARLYON BAY
MARCH
ELVIS COSTELLO
& The Attractions
STATUS QUO
CORNWALL ANTI NUCLEAR
CAMPAIGN BENEFIT
John Williams
& Paco Peña
TWO OF THE WORLD'S
FINEST GUITARISTS
DIRECT FROM THE USA
TOP DISCO FUNK BAND
ROSE ROYCE
THE GREAT JAZZ
BIG BAND SOUND OF
BUDDY
RICH
& His Orchestra
FEATURING DAVE MARCUS
Phase Two improvements
to the Auditorium
MAX
BOYCE
APRIL
Charley
Pride
CLEO LAINE
& The
John Dankworth Quintet
FOUR NIGHTS OF FABULOUS FUN
The
FREDDIE
STARR
SHOW
NOT ONLY TWO CONCERTS
BUT ALSO
TOP-LINE CABARET
RETURNS TO THE WEST
£7.50 INCLUDES BASKET MEAL &
FIRST DRINK FREE
£6.00 NON-DINING TABLE SEAT
£4.50 RESERVED BALCONY SEAT
PLUS FREE ENTRY TO BALLROOM DISCO
MAY PREVIEW
GLEN
CAMPBELL
A STAR AMONG
STARS
SPECIAL GUEST TANYA TUCKER
LEO SAYER
with THE MECHANICS and SPLINTER
Phone PAR 4004

The Jam @ Cornwall Coliseum
25th June 1981
But I'm Different Now
Boy About Town

To Be Someone (Didn't We Have A
Nice Time)
Monday
Man In The Corner Shop
Funeral Pyre
Pretty Green
Private Hell
The Butterfly Collector
Set The House Ablaze
David Watts
Scrape Away
Start!
The Dreams of Children
When You're Young
Little Boy Soldiers
(Love Is Like A) Heat Wave
Going Underground
The Modern World
Strange Town
The Eton Rifles

"I saw the Jam (my favourite band) there in '81...I pushed right to the front to be right in front of Weller.
It was absolutely packed and the pressure from the crowd had made the stage start to buckle upwards. They delayed the start for about 30 or 40 minutes while the road crew got under the stage to try and strap it down and loads of them had to stay there to physically hold it down.
Eventually Weller's old-man (he was their manager) comes on

apologises and introduces them. He walked off and I could see him in the wings saying to Paul Weller and motioning with his hands for them to calm it down. Paul gave him a little cheeky wry smile and they launched into a blistering version of 'Strangetown' and the crowd went mental haha.

You could see the guys under the stage struggling to hold the stage down all through the gig... Still my favourite gig ever."

Kevan Ball (Plymouth)

Siouxsie and the Banshees
@ Cornwall Coliseum
30th July 1981

Israel
Halloween
Paradise Place
Spellbound
Mirage
Tenant
Night Shift
Sin in My Heart
Voodoo Dolly
Christine
Head Cut
Arabian Knights
Eve White / Eve Black
Happy House
Red Over White

Monitor
Love in a Void

"My memories are of my first concerts - the Skids, the Damned and Siouxsie and the Banshees - and of going to the roller disco with my first girlfriend. Time moves on, but a shame Cornwall hasn't got something as wonderful for its current kids as we had growing up."
Tim Sayers (Geelong, Victoria - Australia)

"My 9th birthday treat was Adam and the Ants on his Prince Charming tour - amazing!!! I also saw Ultravox (late 80's) - brilliant!!!"
Jenny Wilson (Cornwall)

Johnny Cash @ Cornwall Coliseum
21st October 1981

Ring of Fire
A Thing Called Love
Folsom Prison Blues
San Quentin
Any Old Wind That Blows
The Last Time
Sunday Mornin' Comin' Down
How Great Thou Art
The Baron
Doin' My Time
Bulle Rider
Streets of Laredo
Riders in the Sky

If I Were a Carpenter
The Wreck of the Old '97
Man in Black
I Walk the Line
Give My Love to Rose
Long Black Veil
Five Feet High and Rising
Big River
Will the Circle Be Unbroken?
Old Flames Can't Hold a Candle
to You
Casey Jones
Orange Blossom Special
A Boy Named Sue

1982

TV was in the news this year with the launching of TSW on the 1st January and the first transmission of CH4 on 2nd November. The very first computer virus 'the Elk Cloner' was written by a 15yr old child, The Falklands war began when Argentina invaded the Falkland Islands, The IRA destroyed a bandstand in London killing 8 soldiers and 7 horses, the very first 'emoticons' were posted, EPCOT was opened in Orlando, the CD player and CD's were launched and the first US lethal injection execution took place in Texas. In the world of entertainment Michael Jackson released 'Thriller', 'ET' was the big movie release of the year and ABBA made their last ever UK TV appearance on the Noel Edmonds Saturday night TV show – ' The Late, Late Breakfast Show'.

Kate Middleton and Prince William were born this year as were Jessica Biel, Kirsten Dunst, Seth Rogan and the 11th Doctor Who Matt Smith. We also lost the great Stanley Holloway, Scottish rock legend Alex Harvey, Ozzy Osbourne's guitarist Randy Rhodes and Captain Mainwaring himself Arthur Lowe and the world of the movies lost the 'legends' Henry Fonda, Ingrid Bergman and Grace Kelly.

The Christmas Number 1 spot went to 'Save Your Love' Renee and Renato and the biggest selling single of the year was by the 're-invented' Dexy's Midnight Runners with 'Come On Eileen'.

"The Cornwall Coliseum was always a great place to play for me and the band, Dr Hook.
The venue was brilliant, people seemed to really love seeing shows there and the audiences were palpably ready to have a great time.
All we had to do was to provide it and it was a great pleasure trying, each and every show.
It was also a lovely bonus to get out of the cities we usually toured

in and be in the terrific Cornwall countryside.
We used to stay at a great big, old hotel in St Austell that had stately rooms and lots of noisy geese, ducks and peacocks (the noisiest!) running around the grounds.
I'm still on the road, so it's sad to see it go, but I'm so proud that Dr Hook is considered a part of the Cornwall Coliseum's colorful history."

Dennis Locorriere (Dr Hook – Vocals/Guitar)

"Luckily played the big hall twice, 1st with Sphinx.
We used flash powder and actually blew the Coliseum trip as it was live & neutral straight through a KO box with fuse wire with the powder poured on top!"

Graham Bath (Sphinx – Guitar)

" I don't recall much at all of the gig, only that it was miles away from any civilization and the rider didn't appear, mind you I haven't been on the memory juice for a while, so something might come to mind !!!!!!!!!!!!"

Algy Ward (Tank – Vocals/Bass)

Whitesnake @ Cornwall Coliseum
11th December '82

Walking In The Shadow of the Blues
Rough an'Ready
Ready an' Willing
Don't Break My Heart Again
Here I Go Again
Lovehunter
Crying In The Rain
Ain't No Love In The Heart of the City
Fool For Your Loving
Thank You Blues
Wine, Women an' Song

"Whitesnake at the Pavilions was always a spectacle and the 'Saints an' Sinners' tour was a great example. Featuring three ex members of Deep Purple - David Coverdale on vocals, Ian Paice on drums and the maestro Jon Lord on keyboards - every show was a bluesy rock masterclass.

The band was probably one of the best at the time and also featured Colin Hodgkinson and Micky Moody on guitar; Moody can now both be seen in the band Snakecharmer, covering Whitesnake classics.

A rowsing version of 'Ain't No Love In The Heart Of The City' had the crowd singing along at the top of their lungs and the band really appreciated it as they always seemed to. All the hits were played too, including – 'Don't Break My Heart Again', 'Fool For Your Loving' and 'Here I Go Again', played in a heavy blues style as this was before Coverdale went 'all American' and filled MTV with 'hair metal' era 'Snake videos.

Ian Carroll (Author –Plymouth)

"I was working one afternoon in the Roller-skating rink sorting out

stuff and a band came in to do their sound check.

One of the band members saw what I was doing and asked me if I could teach him to skate. I said yes and held his hand whilst he made a fool of himself! I didn't realise that the fool was Rick Parfitt from Status Quo!

Big Daddy the wrestler came in to the Wimpy Bar and I got to serve him. He sat with his bum over two seats, one seat for each bum cheek and ordered 2 wimpy special grills. He was very nice and even left me a tip."

Jane Hurley (ex- Cornwall Coliseum staff)

"I can also remember getting the kit in for Status Quo in the early hours of the morning following a gig that had taken place that evening, the plan was that they would the rehearse for the rest of the week and start their tour with two gigs at the coliseum and then go of around the country." **Andy**

Gill (Coliseum Staff, St Austell, Cornwall)

"I went to my very first gig there, I was about 12 maybe 13.

My auntie dropped my friend and I off early so we could get to the front to see Madness.

We were so excited to see them and we did get to the front. When they came on people surged forward and we got really squashed. My friend went to the back and half way through I joined her. It didn't spoil the gig.

They were great. I also saw Cannon and Ball there with my mum and auntie and I think Freddie Starr too "

Sue Lord (Dover, Kent)

"ABC were awful - sounded just like the album "Lexicon of Love" but terrible atmosphere."

Steve Ford (Cornwall)

EUROPEAN HEAVY METAL HEROES
The Sensational
Scorpions
+ SUPPORT
Wed. APRIL 28th
7.30 p.m.
£4.00 ARENA
Cornwall Coliseum

Scorpions @ Cornwall Coliseum
28th April 1982

Blackout
Don't Make No Promises (Your Body
Can't Keep)
Loving You Sunday Morning
Make It Real
We'll Burn the Sky
Coast to Coast
Lovedrive
Always Somewhere
Holiday
Can't Love Without You
He's a Woman – She's a Man
Another Piece of Meat

Dynamite
The Zoo
Steamrock Fever
Can't Get Enough

"I always remember being very excited about going to see the legends of German Heavy Metal – Scorpions – at the Coliseum. My mother, as per usual, paid for my ticket and I was all ready to go, until a few days before the show I came down with a very severe case of chicken pox and so I couldn't go; I was gutted!!! I had to wait until twenty five years later (in 2007) to actually see them at the 'Arrow Rock Festival' in Biddinghuizen, Netherlands, where we were guests as I was due to interview them for the 'From Donington To Download' book that I was writing at the time; due to bad traffic tailbacks I missed the interview, but I did get to see them play, which was well worth the wait."
Ian Carroll (Author, Plymouth)

"The Cornwall Coliseum was where I first saw my first gig Status Quo 1982 was a school night next day couldn't here a thing (ears ringing lol)."
Harry Harris (Torpoint, Cornwall)

"The Shadows did a fantastic show with all the hits they were very talented. I remember Hank Marvin sitting on the front of the stage talking to the audience and saying that they wouldn't have been where they were if not for them.
The audience was very appreciative at the end of the night earning themselves an encore.
The following night David Essex was on and he did not get the same reaction and did not give an encore. (I am not sure if he was there watching the Shadows but the reaction to the audience was very different.)"
Sheila Gill (Usherette – St Austell, Cornwall)

Black Sabbath @ Cornwall Coliseum
14th January '82

E5150
Neon Knights
N.I.B.
Children Of The Sea
Country Girl
Black Sabbath
War Pigs
Slipping Away
Iron Man
The Mob Rules
Heaven and Hell
Paranoid
Children of the Grave

"Having missed Black Sabbath on the 'Heaven And Hell tour' the year before, because I was still at school and still hadn't persuaded my parents to allow me to attend a gig yet, by the time Sabbath came back in January '82, I was more than ready for a bit of Ronnie James Dio and co.

Having been a great Rainbow fan, growing up with Ronnie's vocals, I was ecstatic when he joined Sabbath and preferred him fronting the band to Ozzy – sacrilege some people will say, but I knew what I liked and I feel the same way now.

On 'The Mob Rules Tour' Ronnie ruled the stage as he continued to do for another 28 years, passing away sadly in 2010, but at this time in his career he was a lot younger and very fit and powerful.

Featuring a mix of songs from 'Heaven and Hell', 'The Mob Rules' and Ronnie's take on the Sabbath classics, the show was a huge hit and I bought a t-shirt, as I always seemed to at every concert I went to, thanks to money from my mother – I was a little spoilt for clothing.

It was another excellent show and secured my belief that Mr Dio was one of the greatest singers ever.

(As a side note, Ronnie rang me at home in my kitchen when I was doing interviews for my book 'From Donington to Download' 27 years later, a week before he cancelled his final UK tour and around six months before he passed away; in 2012 I went to LA and visited his tomb in Forest Lawn Memorial Park, a more peaceful place you'll never find.)

Ian Carroll (Author, Plymouth)

"My parents had a small guest house, the groupies from Black Sabbath stayed, they totally trashed the rooms, but they did give us some merchandise!!

After they stayed my parents were really wary of who knocked on the door."

Nancy (St Blazey, Cornwall)

"Vera Lynn performed at a commemorative concert I can't remember what for but I can remember a lot of the audience were proudly displaying their medals and thoroughly enjoyed the night."

Sheila Gill (Usherette – St Austell, Cornwall)

"The Coliseum for many years provided a method of enjoyment and relief from depression. As a totally deaf person, I was unable obviously to hear all the groups that I attended and the unmentionable number of nights at Quasars, Bentleys and the Ocean Suite.

Luckily for myself and other deaf friends who frequented the clubs and events, the dance floors were wood, which is a fabulous conductor of sound, and therefore the floors would vibrate and we would all be able to feel the beat and join in. Deaf people get very depressed at times with their situation, which there is no way out of. But having such a glorious setting to spend evenings in and being able to mix in almost (some of us used sign language so we did stick out a wee bit), unnoticed by the majority and have a really good time.

My best evening had to be Status Quo, where I was standing (or rather jumping and rolling my head) right next to the speakers. The vibrations from them were out of this world! Everyone else at the end of the evening was like myself Totally Deaf. What fun…."

Stephen Nott (St Austell, Cornwall)

"The following January I went to see the "Redrocker" himself Sammy Hagar (supported by Grand Prix) on his 'Standing Hampton' tour.

This time I remember the large car park and inside the venue the various pillars which was part of the construction of the venue.

Sammy Hagar opened up with 'Heavy Metal' the title track to the soundtrack of the animated film of the same name.

I remember Hagar running up and down the stack of amps, which stood high either side of the stage, playing his Red Gibson Explorer guitar.
This was to be the best concert I ever attended at the coliseum."
Mark Jewitt (Plymouth, Devon)

"Still the best gig of my life, was Sammy Hagar. His showmanship, fantastic backing band, energy and most of all, the sound.
It was so loud yet absolutely crystal clear... Amazing!"
Theo Christian (Gateshead)

"I've just been listening to my latest acquisition 'The Circle At Your Service' and it reminded me of seeing Sammy Hagar at the Coliseum. I can't remember the exact year it was around 1980 and was the 'Standing Hampton' tour.
I had bought the 'Street Machine' album and had to see this guy.
He was awesome running around the stage jumping off the speaker stacks etc. What sticks in my mind was mid concert he said he was going to do something he normally didn't do and cover another bands song. He was only doing this because that band had recently played for the final time, the song he played was 'Whole Lotta Love', it was a great cover close to the original and as a Led Zeppelin fan who would never get the chance to see them live it was amazing to hear an all time favourite played in true Led Zeppelin style. The whole gig was awesome."
Steve Humphreys (Torpoint, Cornwall)

Duran Duran @ Cornwall Coliseum
22nd November 1982

Rio
Hungry Like the Wolf
Last Chance on the Stairway
Lonely in Your Nightmare
Sound of Thunder
Night Boat
New Religion

Friends of Mine
Save A Prayer
Planet Earth
Hold Back the Rain
Careless Memories
Make Me Smile (Come Up –
and See Me)
My Own Way
Girls on Film

"Once I'd finished at college, where incidentally, Heather McNally had also been studying – the same subject as me, BA (Hons) Graphic Design - although she was a year above, I continued to work at the Coliseum.
In 1982, I found my first job as an Artworker/Graphic Designer, at Tanhoit, Wheal Northey. It was Tanhoit that designed and printed the many promotional leaflets for the Coliseum. In fact, they'd also been responsible for the now familiar logos. The Coliseum wasn't going to let me go, just yet, and I still continued to work there, mainly roller-skating, for another year."
Martyn (aka Skippy) Feather (Lancing, Sussex)

"My dad Brian Kelley used to take the money on the car park there. He so loved his job and died way too early at 58.
I also have great memories of seeing The Who, Thin Lizzy, Robert Plant, Whitesnake, Gillan, Motorhead (of whom we listened to their soundcheck whilst lying on the beach, lol) and many other bands who we are still going to see now."
Sue Williams (Ulley, Sheffield)

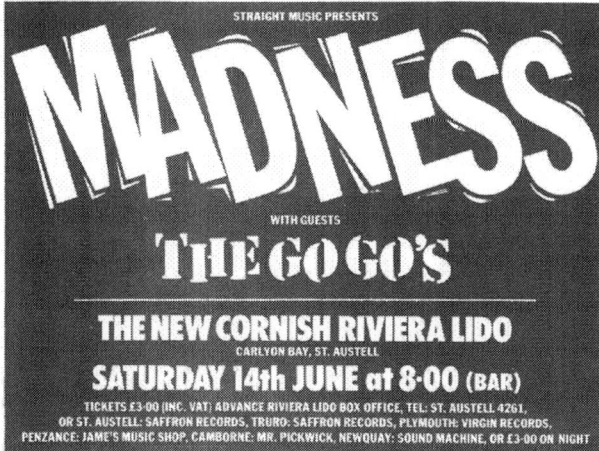

STRAIGHT MUSIC PRESENTS

MADNESS

WITH GUESTS

THE GO GO'S

THE NEW CORNISH RIVIERA LIDO
CARLYON BAY, ST. AUSTELL

SATURDAY 14th JUNE at 8·00 (BAR)

TICKETS £3·00 (INC. VAT) ADVANCE RIVIERA LIDO BOX OFFICE, TEL: ST. AUSTELL 4261,
OR ST. AUSTELL: SAFFRON RECORDS, TRURO: SAFFRON RECORDS, PLYMOUTH: VIRGIN RECORDS,
PENZANCE: JAME'S MUSIC SHOP, CAMBORNE: MR. PICKWICK, NEWQUAY: SOUND MACHINE, OR £3·00 ON NIGHT

"First time I went was when myself, my cousin plus both our mothers and a coach full of skinheads went to see Madness there. Just before the coach left to come back my mother and I were sat watching out the window as a rather pissed skinhead relieved himself over the wheel arch below us."

Steven Moore (Plymouth, Devon)

"I have several programs and photos from when I went to the Coliseum I saw Showaddywaddy 4 times, the Who, Elton John, Tight Fit, Bucks Fizz 3 times, Thin Lizzy, The Four Tops, The Temptations, The Drifters, the Everley Brothers, Don Williams, Jim Davison, Jethro, Madness, the Three Degrees, Leo Sayer, Shakey, The Shadows, Hot Chocolate, Freddie Starr.
I remember the Madness gig where there was an all mighty fight at the front of the stage and someone was stabbed all Madness did was mess about. But the Three Degrees were very bad.
I saw Sabbath there but I don't remember Ozzy being there.
Saw the Harlem Globetrotters there and they were brilliant that's all the groups I remember, ok 1 more Kid Creole and the Coconuts! Missed Tina Turner ex missus's car broke down…"

Steve Pearce (Newquay, Cornwall)

"I went to my very first gig there.
I was about 12 maybe 13, my auntie dropped my friend and I off early so we could get to the front to see Madness. We were so excited to see them and we did get to the front.
When they came on people surged forward and we got really

squashed, my friend went to the back and half way through I joined her, it didn't spoil the gig. They were great.
Also saw Cannon and Ball there with my mum and auntie and I think Freddie Starr too."
Sue Lord (Dover, Kent)

"One of the best gigs I remember going to was Ozzy Osbourne on the 'Speak of the Devil' tour December 10th 1982.
I went with my good friend Del Hodd & getting carried away with the atmosphere we got into buying pints of beer & then tipping them over each other's heads!!?? Beer was cheap in those days.
I went home with a tour poster, which was a bonus.
Brilliant night although disappointed Ozzy had been stopped from having dwarves on stage at this point."
John Marsh (St Austell, Cornwall)

Slade @ Cornwall Coliseum
14th December '82

Rock and Roll Preacher
When I'm Dancin' I Ain't Fightin'
Take Me Bak 'Ome
And Now The Waltz (C'est La Vie)
Far Far Away
A Night To Remember
Lock Up Your Daughters
Gudbuy T'Jane
We'll Bring the House Down
Get Down and Get With It
Mama Weer All Crazee Now
Merry Christmas Everybody

"Slade were one of my favourite bands from my youth and when I was still at primary school I learnt all their songs off by heart.
The chance to see Noddy, Dave, Don and Jimmy, up close and personal, was a dream come true.
Being just before Christmas as well made it even more special when they sang 'Merry Christmas Everybody'.
Slade were back on form after a few years in the wilderness – they were 'surprise guests at Reading '80 and their career just picked up again after that and the hits hard started up all over again.
The venue was packed and they put on a brilliant show, sadly that was to be the only time that I saw the full line-up of Slade, Noddy and Jimmy both leaving before I saw them again at Butlins in 2015."

Ian Carroll (Author, Plymouth)

"Being very impressed by Slade live."

Theo Christian (Gateshead)

"Gillan at the Coliseum was always a great show and being a fairly young rocker, as were my friends, we always looked forward to the inevitable encore of the Deep Purple favourite 'Smoke On The Water', which at the time was still Ian Gillan's previous band; this was before the short stint for one album and one tour with Black Sabbath and before the triumphant return to fronting the 'Purps'.
I remember the support one time being the Welsh legends Budgie who always put on an amazing show, especially for a three piece.
Unfortunately I had missed Gillan with Bernie Tormé - the young crazy loose cannon on the block - but the replacement was Janick Gers who came to Gillan from White Spirit and was a flamboyant and more than respectable replacement; Janick went on to join Iron Maiden and he's still with them now.
Gillan churned out the 'hits' in the shape of 'New Orleans', 'Trouble' and more. The show was one of the best at the time at the Coliseum and always sold out."

Ian Carroll (Author –Plymouth)

"Status Quo concerts were arena gigs and the audience were packed in. When you worked on the balconies and the audience were jumping in unison it looked like you could have walked from one side of the arena to the other."

Sheila Gill (Usherette – St Austell, Cornwall)

"I remember coming to watch lots of bands with friends and with my mum, Dexy's, my heartthrob David Cassidy, but the most important was Dr Hook, my Mums favourite band, took her to see them a few months before she passed away in 1982. She enjoyed it so much.

Also, we always went into the Wimpy, to have something to eat while the traffic cleared, good times."

Janet Dicker (Plymouth, Devon)

"The first time I saw Ozzy was in 1982 at the Coliseum with Waysted - featuring Pete Way of UFO - as support.

I'd always preferred Ozzy on his own and Sabbath with Dio and I still do.

This tour was the first not to feature Randy Rhoads who had died in a light airplane crash in the March of this year. The temporary replacement for Ozzy's guitarist virtuoso was Brad Gillis of the American AOR band 'Nightranger' and he fitted in really well as a 'stop gap guitarist' until the arrival of Jake E Lee.

Waysted came and went, filling the support slot as best they could, but the crowd were there for Ozzy.

With an Ozzy solo show you always get the best of Black Sabbath and the best of his solo stuff, so the crowd lapped it up.

Ozzy had very short cropped hair at this show as his hair was just growing back from when he'd shaved his head, so he looked virtually unrecognisable from the Ozzy we know today."

Ian Carroll (Author –Plymouth)

"I am a St Austell girl born and bred but moved to Wiltshire 3 years ago.

I was born in 1951, so my great memories are mostly in the middle to late 1960's (I wasn't really old enough to be there but no one worried too much then) after that I moved on to the Blue Lagoon in Newquay, as did a lot of us! My son Richard Winterburn has encouraged me to write to you.

I am a real music fan, I saw the Beatles in Plymouth when I was a very young teenager! I went to Crinnis to see people like Herman's Hermits, the Searchers, Long John Baldry, PJ Proby and many more but I do remember Reg Presley of the Troggs getting caught up with his microphone lead around his neck and taking a dive into the audience, obviously he survived but it was very frightening.

I also remember that fights always seemed to break out at the end of the evening, St Austell was quite well known for this.

The other thing I can say, although not particularly complementary, was that through my job I hired a car to Status Quo in 1982 (?) when they used the venue to rehearse for their forthcoming World Tour.

They were there for a week. The road manager had to hire the car because the insurance company would not hire to musicians. They were not happy about that.

I delivered the car, and was asked to wait, I didn't mind because I got to watch them rehearsing, after half an hour their manager *came and I handed over the car (a Ford Granada).*

Some of my colleagues had previously asked if I could get their albums signed. The manager said he would see what he could do. I collected the car from the Fowey Hotel on the Sunday. I took my 4-year-old son Richard with me because it was my day off and I had no child-minder. Status Quo were all sat around talking, laughing and the albums were given back to me unsigned. I asked if they could sign but was ushered out saying they were too busy. Rick Parfitt even let the door slam in our faces when he barged passed us. Not a very nice man in my opinion.

My lasting impression of Status Quo is that they were arrogant and had a total disregard for the fans that had spent their hard earned money to buy their LPs."

Trudy Winterburn (Trowbridge, Wiltshire)

Saxon @ Cornwall Coliseum
14th January '82

Motorcycle Man
Princess of the Night
Never Surrender

Hungry Years
20,000Ft
The Eagle Has Landed
Heavy Metal Thunder
Strong Arm of the Law
747 (Strangers in the Night)
Wheels of Steel
Dallas 1pm
Suzie Hold On
Denim and Leather

"The first time that I ever saw Saxon was at the Coliseum with my friend Theo. For some reason we caught the train down, but arrived really early around lunchtime.

We mucked about for most of the afternoon, hanging around the back entrance to the Coliseum and listening to the soundcheck through the open backdoors. At various points through the afternoon we met various members of the band and I got autographs and Theo managed to get an autographed drum lid, which seemed pretty unbelievable at the time.

When the gig started we watched the support Cheetah from the barrier, they were fronted by two 'rock chicks' big hair and tight jeans - Chrissie and Lyndsay Hammond - and they were very much in AC/DC vein, especially as they came from Australia as well, with a bit of Meat Loaf style songs thrown in for good measure. They were fresh from an appearance at Reading Festival the month before and very popular with the males in the audience, which in those days at 'metal' shows seemed to be around 90% of the audience. After this tour I never heard of Cheetah again, so I don't know what happened to them, they could be playing pubs to this day in Oz, such a shame for a band with some initial potential.

Then it was time for Saxon. The tour was supporting their first 'live' album 'The Eagle Has Landed' which had been a top ten album when released four months earlier and so was a set full of classics.

We were treated to songs including '747 Strangers In The Night', 'Motorcycle Man', 'Princess of the Night' and of course 'Wheels of Steel' and we all loved it.

After the show we walked back to St Austell train station, which is quite a walk, to find out that there were no trains until the morning, so we took turns sitting on the seat in the photo booth, with the 'half curtain' pulled across - which made no difference to stopping the wind, it was a bizarre end to an amazing day. Good times!!!"

Ian Carroll (Author, Plymouth)

"The first memory is the day out Ian (the Author) and I went to see Saxon.

We spent the day hanging around whilst the roadies prepared the stage and spoke to the drum roadie who gave me the skin of the snare drum, which had been battered during the sound-check. After the gig I managed to get it signed by the band, but I no longer have it as it too got 'tidied' by my dad.

Ian and I went to a lot of gigs there together and I always remember it being a great occasion, getting the coach from Plymouth as Virgin Records sold a travel/ticket combo, which was great for us non drivers."

Theo Christian (Gateshead)

"As a young and budding DJ in the St Austell area at the end of the 70's I was hoping to become a professional DJ.

Moving from St Austell YMCA and then to my own roadshow I was hoping to get the chance to work at Bentleys, I loved CC, I was taught to swim there by Surfing world champion Graham Nile and had spent a lot of my childhood on the beach.

At the end of 1981 I finally plucked up courage to ask at the Coliseum and was given a chance by the McNally's, firstly in the roller disco and then at the start of 1982 some Friday nights at Bentley's.

How much fun it was to DJ at a roller disco. People skating in a circle at the same tempo as the music that's playing. Just for fun we used to play really fast songs, get people up to speed and then shout in the mic "Everyone turn around and skate in the opposite direction". The result being a pile up between the good skaters at the front who turned quickly and the bad skaters at the back who didn't! It was heaven!

But it was short lived as I had also applied for full time work for Juliana's of London, at the time one of the world's biggest DJ agencies, sending DJ's all over the world. This was a company

that former Coliseum DJ Andy Munroe had worked for. I got the job and of course I took it.
I travelled Europe and settled in Norway where 33 years later I sill DJ at clubs and festivals. I cherish the memories of those few months of playing at CC, and am grateful for the chance I was given there. Concerts with Japan, Blancmange, Elvis Costello, The Specials and The Swinging Cats were my favourites."
Chris Shepherd (Bodo, Norway)

Ultravox @ Cornwall Coliseum
18th December 1982

Reap The Wild Wind
When the Scream Subsides
The Thin Wall
New Europeans
We Stand Alone
I Remember (Death in the Afternoon)
Visions In Blue
Mr. X
Sleepwalk
The Voice
Vienna
Astradyne
All Stood Still
Passing Strangers
Mine for Life
Hymn

The Song (We Go)

Budgie @ Cornwall Coliseum
10th December 1982

Hold on to Love

Truth Drug
Crime Against the World
Flowers in the Attic
Superstar
She Used Me Up
In for the Kill
Rape of the Locks
Breadfan

Genesis @ Cornwall Coliseum
18th September 1982

Dance on a Volcano
Behind the Lines

Follow You Follow Me
Dodo/Lurker
Abacab
Supper's Ready
Misunderstanding
Man on the Corner
Who Dunnit?
In the Cage
The Cinema Show
The Colony of Slippermen
Afterglow
Turn It On Again
Los Endos
The Lamb Lies Down on Broadway
Watcher of the Skies
I Know What I Like (In Your Wardrobe)

1983

This year got off to a great start with 'Fraggle Rock' broadcast for the first time on TV worldwide, Motown celebrated its 25th Anniversary with a TV special and Michael Jackson 'moonwalked' for the first time on the show, the Japanese Disneyland opened in Tokyo and 'Return Of The Jedi' opened in cinemas.

Margaret Thatcher was re-elected with a landslide majority, Nazi war criminal Klaus Barbie was arrested in Bolivia, rock legends KISS appeared on MTV for the first time ever WITHOUT their make-up, 'Wheel Of Fortune' began nationally in the USA, Neil Kinnock became leader of the Labour Party and the Brink's-MAT robbery took place in their vault at Heathrow Airport – 6,800 gold bars were stolen worth £26 million and only a fraction of the gold was ever retrieved.

In the world of superheroes both the actors who played Thor – Chris Hemsworth and Andrew Garfield who portrayed Spiderman were born. In the music world Amy Winehouse, Professor Green and Taylor Hanson – of Hanson – were born. This year also saw the deaths of British comedy legend Dick Emery, quintessential English actor David Niven, Beach Boys co-founder Dennis Wilson and Barney Bubbles who was a graphic designer and music video director who produced album and single covers for amongst many - Ian Dury and the Blockheads, Hawwind, The Damned and Elvis Costello and also directing the videos for 'Ghost Town' by The Specials, 'Is That Love?' by Squeeze and 'The Lunatics (Have Taken Over The Asylum)' by Fun Boy Three.
The best selling single of the year went to 'Karma Chameleon' by Culture Club and the Christmas number one spot was filled with the vocal classic 'Only You' by The Flying Pickets.

"We have such fantastic memories of spending two weeks in the summer of 1983 at The Coliseum in Cornwall.
The weather was glorious every day. I remember jet skiing, partying most every night and having the most amazing audiences for every performance at The Coliseum.
What a wonderful time we had there and a time that we will always remember."

Cheryl, Mike and Jay (formerly of Bucks Fizz)

"We played at Cornwall Coliseum in St. Austell on my 25th birthday.
Then we all went after load out, on the tour bus and we ended up in Plymouth at a restaurant to celebrate my birthday.
The tour manager had steaks flown in for my birthday, the

restaurant cooked the steaks for every one in my crew and in my
band we drank Champagne and celebrated.
Randy Castillo was in the band at the time."
Lita Ford (Vocals/Guitar)

Rainbow @ Cornwall Coliseum
September 19th 1983

Spotlight Kid
MISS Mistreated
Fool For The Night
I Surrender
Can't Happen Here
Catch The Rainbow
Drinking With The Devil
Difficult To Cure
Power
Stranded
Death Alley Driver
Fire Dance
All Night Long
Since You Been Gone
Long Live Rock 'n' Roll
Hey Joe / Smoke On The Water
Kill The King

"The second time I saw Rainbow at the Coliseum was on the 'Bent
Out of Shape' tour and as expected was another great gig and this
time the support was amazing as before too.
Rainbow treated us to many hits covering all three versions of the
band and the support Lita Ford ex of all girl band the Runaways
was amazing, destroying the crowd with hot licks, upon roaring

solos.

I even bought a brilliant three quarter length sleeved baseball jersey with Lita on the front and dates on the back - never know what happened to that though...?"

Ian Carroll (Author –Plymouth)

"I have to confess I have no memories of playing that venue at all I'm afraid! Sorry. Good luck with the book though."

Mark King (Level 42 – Vocals/Bass)

"2nd time was with my new band Persian Risk, had a call from Bob Sanderson to support Motorhead in July 83' funnily enough Phil Campell was the other guitarist with me in Risk and a year later joined the Head!!!!

Great times, great venue."

Graham Bath (Persian Risk – Guitar)

"I finally said good-bye to the Coliseum in 1983, when I moved to a new job, as studio manager in a small advertising agency, in Newbury, Berkshire.

Six very happy years, six years I will never forget."

Martyn (aka Skippy) Feather (Lancing, Sussex)

"I know it has been mentioned about one of the bar staff having his Reliant Robin thrown in the pool however the next morning after it had been lifted out there remained an oil mark around the edge of the pool. So two of us borrowed wetsuits from the windsurfing school that were operating there and were given cleaning materials and spent hours in a very cold pool cleaning the marks off." Andy

Gill (Coliseum Staff, St Austell, Cornwall)

"I still have the reference that Bill Search wrote for me dated Dec 1983.

My daughter had her 16th birthday party in the Ocean Suite; I had my 30th birthday put up in lights on the board.

We have been to many shows Tina Turner, Dr. Hook, Leo Sayer, Hot Chocolate, Gladys Knight and the Pips to name but a few, WOMAD of course what an experience we will never see the like of here again.

I am a local girl so I have many happy memories both of the place itself and the staff that worked there, what a tragedy its now all gone, but never forgotten."

Shirley Penrose (Fowey, Cornwall)

"It was cold and it was November, but that didn't stop me having a fiery passion in my loins. Before PIL took to the stage I and my girlfriend at the time, went out into the car park and went behind a hut and had sex on a large sign that was laying on the ground saying 'Welcome to Cornish Leisureworld' – the performance by PIL was a lot better, I blame the cold wind for my performance."

Ian Carroll (Author)

"Me and some mates saw Big Country in '83 when they were at the height of their popularity.
It was rammed full and when they played 'Chance' the whole crowd jumped up and down through the song and you could feel the floor flexing like a trampoline...awesome."

Kevan Ball (Plymouth)

"Going to see Wham! was simply embarrassing, although I think it was after that gig that I got into a daft fight with one of my mates in the car park!!"

Steve Ford (Cornwall)

"On another occasion I had to take some punk rockers from Plymouth to the Coliseum to see Johnny Rotten on a very dark winters night. Thinking there could be problems, I asked the local Police for some sort of escort but they could not help.
However things went very well on the outward and return journey until I got back to the depot and had to clean the coach. They had been inhaling glue through straws, you have never seen such a mess what with all the vomit and empty glue cans!"

Peter Lucas (Plymouth, Devon)

"My parents owned the petrol station at Tideford (Riverside Garage) at the time I was a huge Bucks Fizz fan, I was in love with Bobby G!!
I was at the petrol station one day and my mum called me into the shop and there was Bobby G from Bucks Fizz, he said hello to me and my sister and signed autographs for us on the hand written petrol receipt pad (if only it was in the day of mobile phones with cameras!).
I was completely star struck didn't say a word.
My mum then told me that we had tickets for their concert that, night down the Cornwall Coliseum, it was 1983. I was 9yrs old.
The memory that sticks in my mind for every concert was the traffic and the snail pace queue winding round the car park before climbing up the huge hill!"

Julie Smith (Plymouth, Devon)

"Roller disco's, U16 disco, U16 Friday evening Baby "Bentleys", for us up and coming wannabe Mod's.
The start of seeing pop groups, real life pop stars!!!! Aged 11,

when myself and my best mate Debbie went to see Shaking Stevens, it was her 11th birthday!! Adam and the Ants, Bucks Fizz, Kid Creole and the Coconuts, Van Morrison, Status Quo, James, The Commitments and many more."

Tami Cross-Halls (St Austell, Cornwall - Aged 43 & 3/4)

"Evening roller disco. Over 90% couldn't skate. Let alone dance. Fumbling around the edges, gripping on for dear life. Bumping into the bar area where in very heavy shorts glasses the drink of choice, (after a few obligatory lager & limes) was vodka & limes or Southern Comfort."

Denis Bennett (St Austell, Cornwall)

"Gillan, was also in 1983. I think it was when I had the famous 'magical mystery tour' in the boot of the car, as I bought the last ticket to the gig in Virgin records Armada way, Plymouth."

Harry Harris (Torpoint, Cornwall)

"Freddie Starr picked me out of the audience and hauled me up onto the stage to sit me on a chair and it gave me strong electric shocks.
Then he placed my head in some guillotine type stocks and pretended to behead me and in the end half a cucumber fell into a bucket below my head on the stage much to the 3000 odd crowd's entertainment!
I'm sure Freddie Starr was pissed whilst performing but it was all very funny!"

Lee Slaughter (St Austell)

"The day that we went to see Motorhead on the 'Another Perfect Day' tour, it was a perfect day. It was July 3rd and a venue sunny day, so we went first up onto Plymouth Hoe (we lived in Plymouth) and got very drunk on 'Blue Curacao' – not sure who else went with us apart from my friend Theo Christian and I think Rob Lintern, but by the time we arrived at the Pavilions we were all wasted.

This was the first time for me to watch Motorhead and the last tour that featured Phil 'Philthy Animal' Taylor and the short lived Motorhead career of Brian 'Robbo' Robertson (ex Thin Lizzy) as they both left shortly after.

But the show was amazing, what I remember of it and the crowd were up for it."

Ian Carroll (Author)

"Not being able to walk straight for a couple of days after being at the front during the Motörhead gig."

Chris Martin-Gathern (Dikanäs, Västerbottens Län, Sweden)

"The second time that I saw Thin Lizzy was on the 'Thunder & Lightning' tour which featured new guitarist John Sykes.
Sykes had been the guitarist in the Tygers of Pan Tang, so I had seen him at my first ever gig at the Coliseum two years before.
Lizzy were on top form, playing all the classics plus a few tracks from the new album, little did we know that they would be playing their final UK show as the original band only 5 months later when they headlined Reading Festival.
I also managed to find a plectrum that night, which I gave to my friend Theo's sister Debra as I already had one from the previous 'Renegade' tour – I'm kind like that."

Ian Carroll (Author, Plymouth)

"I remember going to watch Thin Lizzy with my brother and his mate Ian. At the end of the gig the guitarist threw his plectrum into the audience, my brothers mate caught it and gave it to me.
I kept it for years in my jewellery box, fond memories."

Debra Heron (Plymouth, Devon)

"At Thin Lizzy I shook Scott Gorham's Hand in front row on the 'Thunder and Lightning' tour."
Harry Harris (Torpoint, Cornwall)

"I went to see Thin Lizzy at the Coliseum back in 1983 on their final tour.
After the concert me and a load of me mates went round the back hoping to catch a glimpse of the band leaving the building and Phil Lynott came out worse for wear and fell down the full flight of stairs and got up in a temper, kicked the wing mirror from the car that was waiting to take them away. Someone eventually from the Lizzy gang eventually gave him a pill or something to calm down, and he got in the car and they all left.
It left us all shocked at the time.
If you look closely on the DVD of one of the gigs that followed that concert which was recorded in Dublin you could still see a big bruise on his arm, which of course was famously caused at our very own Coliseum.
I'm a big fan of Thin Lizzy so it's not something me and fans talk about cause we didn't want to see our favourite rock star in such a way, but I felt I had to mention it."
Dave Knight (Bugle, Cornwall)

"I met Lynott once, after their gig at the Cornwall Coliseum on the farewell Lizzy tour in 1983. After queuing for autographs and a sight of the band I performed the ritual I performed after every gig there... I phoned my dad to come and pick me up and passed the good half hour wait while he drove from Truro to St Austell to fetch me mooching around the site. Bored, I wandered back into the empty hall (as I usually did) to watch the roadies break down the set. Suddenly Philo appeared from backstage carrying a half empty Smirnoff bottle and clocked this forlorn teenager in a huge empty hall. He asked, "What's up, you OK?" And when I explained I was just waiting for my lift he beckoned me up on stage and said, "Well, you can wait up here if you like." So for the next twenty minutes or so we sat side by side on Brian Downey's drum riser chatting about this or that and shooting the breeze. Talking about music, stuff we liked, Phil's plans post-Lizzy. He really seemed like a genuinely lovely, soft spoken (slightly drunk) guy. Bless him, he was still in full stage apparel and was dangling his legs back and forth. He was mortified when he accidentally kicked my shin with his big cowboy boots and apologised the way only a cheerfully half

cut person can. Eventually dad appeared at far end of the hall, wondering where I was. I bade Phil farewell and jumped down off the stage before heading home. So, for so many reasons, I guess, Phil will always be my number one bass hero."
Trevor Raggatt (London)

"Thin Lizzy, not long before Lynott died, The Cult, Echo and the Bunnymen, PIL, New Model Army, the Ramones, ABC, the list goes on. I often find myself remembering another band I'd forgotten I saw there. We were extremely lucky to have it, then later I was at Gossips every weekend as well!"
Mike Bennett (Cornwall)

"I was doing a ceramics course at Cornwall College and I think I was waiting for a bus to go home when a friend stopped and said, "do you want to come to the Coliseum?" So I just jumped on the back of his bike and off we went.
I was covered in clay but I didn't care - the band was Thin Lizzy!! One of the best nights there (and there were many!!)"
Sue Thompson (Falmouth, Cornwall)

"Thin Lizzy 1983, 'Thunder & Lightning' tour! The Greatest Band ever! I was bursting with excitement knowing I was going to see them!
Motörhead seeing Lemmy in the flesh!
Great times such a shame."
Tracey J Courage (Truro, Cornwall)

Gary Numan @ Cornwall Coliseum
November 2nd 1983

Sister Surprise
Warriors
Remind Me To Smile
Metal
This Prison Moon
Down In The Park

Films
She's Got Claws
Love Needs No Disguise
I Die, You Die
Love Is Like Clock Law
The Iceman Comes
The Rhythm of the Evening
This Is My House
I Am Render
War Songs
My Centurion
The Tick Tock Man
We Take Mystery (To Bed)
Cars
Are 'Friends' Electric?
Tracks
We Are Glass

"The Gary Numan concert in '83 was one of the few that I attended on my own, most of my friends being 'Rock & Metal Heads'.
Gary Numan was amazing and at the time I didn't know that I would be interviewing him in person, twenty two years later for my book 'Music, Mud and Mayhem: The Official History of the Reading Festival'.
The show was very 'polished' and sold out. Everyone left really pleased."
Ian Carroll (Author)

"Culture Club - there was a big delay in the band coming on stage as Boy George refused to perform until all the illegal merchandise sellers outside the Coliseum were removed!!"

Lee Slaughter (St Austell)

"I never did like Led Zeppelin, they did absolutely nothing for me. I made the fatal mistake once of saying that I was 'gutted' when my girlfriend at the time told me that the Robert Plant show at the Coliseum was sold out. She came back to me a week later to tell me that she had got me a ticket to see him and that we were going.
It was the 'Big Log' tour and it was as dull as the album. My fault for opening my big mouth…."

Ian Carroll (Author)

"Danny from 'Fame' was my heart throb although looking back now I wouldn't think the same, I remember going to the Cornwall Coliseum just after Danny from the 'Kids From Fame' had released the single "Friday Night's Gonna Be Alright".
I was sat quite far back at this concert and to be fair I wouldn't of known whether it was the cast from the TV show or not, I just remember lots of Lycra & leg warmers. Leeroy in his sweatband and the grand finale "Fame" - I'm gonna live forever I'm gonna learn how to fly!!! No, I'm not - I'm going to end up working in an office! Lol!!"

Julie Smith (Plymouth, Devon)

"The best concert ever.,. The Kids From Fame!!! Yes, honestly. Not sure which year early 80's. Went with my younger sister, it was just so exciting especially at the end we all went outside round the back to wait to see some of them come out to see us. The TV show was absolutely massive at the time - we felt like we were so special going to see them live and just down the road."

Alison Pearson (Nr Exeter, Devon)

"I also made full use of the Roller Disco on Saturday afternoons, there were a group of older Scouts from Polkerris who got together and formed a group of older members, and we were there every Saturday. Great memories."

Stephen Nott (St Austell, Cornwall)

"Just fond memories of being a kid growing up in Cornwall.
The Coliseum was our first taste of independence, being dropped off by parents with Yoyo Hamblen for what seemed like hours and hours of fun to roller skate primarily and hang out in the arcades.

Always so much fun and always finished off with a trip to the Wimpy!"

Rob Hamblen (Dubai)

"They were all bands I went to see between the ages of 15 & 18.
I would have to get a coach from Exeter to Cornwall, I remember that first time we got off the bus and thought wow its huge, made me feel very grown up lol,
Kajagoogoo I couldn't see very well so I asked the bloke in front if I could sit on his shoulders which he did, I was a lot smaller then!"

Sharon Elston (Exeter, Devon)

"I had the pleasure of attending the Cornwall Coliseum when the enigmatic and flamboyant Boy George brought his band Culture Club to the venue at the height of his popularity, on a crest of a wave, in the early 80's.
The crowd were ecstatic, the young followers and curious rockers mesmerised by the enchanting sound that epitomised a long gone era of pop mania, with style and charisma.
Nobody wanted to hurt Boy George, testimony has shown it was all self inflicted, nevertheless 2015 has seen a triumphant return of a troubled soul. The echoes can still be heard in the crashing waves of nostalgia as the moonlight kisses the bay, to be clever of course!"

Paul Paskins (Plymouth, Devon)

1984

This twelve month spell began with the start of a year long 'Miners Strike', Marvin Gaye was shot to death by his father – the first shot was fatal and through his heart, 'Terms of Endearment' won 5 Oscars including Best Picture, Tommy Cooper collapsed and died live on TV and scientists in the US announced that they had discovered the AIDS Virus.

Bruce Springsteen released his classic album 'Born In The USA', it was revealed that GCSE's would take the place of O-Levels and CSE's, France won Euro '84, the Olympics were held in Los Angeles where Zola Budd - running for the UK - collided with the US runner Mary Decker destroying both their medal winning chances and British Telecom was privatized.

In football Arjen Robben, Carlos Tevez and Fernando Torres were all born. Elswhere in the world Katy Perry, Prince Harry and Mark Zuckerberg – the founder of Facebook – were all born as well. The world mourned the deaths of Johnny Weissmuller who played 'Tarzan' throughout the 1930's and 40's, Diana Dors, Richard Burton and the assassinated Indian Prime Minister Indira Gandhi.

The best selling single of the year in the UK and the Christmas number one were a 'charity double' by 'Do They Know It's Christmas?' by Band Aid, masterminded by Bob Geldof to raise money for the starving millions in Ethiopia.

"Cornwall Coliseum was the venue for my third gig with KISS! I was thrilled with my new job as lead guitarist for "The Hottest Band in the Land, KISS!" but honestly, the first week or so of my being in the band was very nerve-racking.
I know I was prepared, but I was not that familiar with the way Gene Simmons and Paul Stanley would command the stage. We always enjoyed the opening act Bon Jovi, and this was way before

they became world famous. I was really thrilled touring in the UK, since the British Invasion was so important to me growing up loving music and dreaming of being a famous guitarist.

After viewing the photos of the venue it looks familiar but not in anyway that I can relate a story to the actual venue, I regret that now that is lost!

I hope it's history will be memorialized and I now I can say, I played there, early in my KISSTORY."

Bruce Kulick (KISS – Lead Guitar)

KISS @ Cornwall Coliseum
October 2nd 1984

Detroit Rock City
Cold Gin
Strutter
Fits Like a Glove
Under The Gun
Heaven's on Fire
War Machine
Young and Wasted
I've Had Enough (Into The Fire)
I Still Love You
Lick It Up
I Love It Loud
Love Gun
Rock and Roll All Nite

Creatures of the Night
Black Diamond

"One of my favourite bands of all time, for KISS to play so near to where I lived was unbelievable when they headlined the Coliseum

on the 'Animalize' tour. With their 'brand new' guitarist Bruce Kulick having just joined to replace the ill Mark St John.

The support band was a new band that I had heard of on the 'Friday Rock Show', a little band from New Jersey called Bon Jovi. Jon Bon Jovi, complete with a string vest and the curliest of shaggy perms, lead his band through tracks from the first album that was yet to be released, they went down well, but not as well as KISS.

Performing all the classics and some tracks from the new 'Animalize' album, KISS were still in their 'without make-up' stage and so were 'glammed up' with their clothes instead.

A brilliant night of American rock 'n' roll and the only time that KISS has ever played in Cornwall."

Ian Carroll (Author)

"I met Gene Simmons and Paul Stanley from KISS when they were at the Cornwall Coliseum; I even got to strum the axe of Simmons and was invited to the after show at the Holiday Inn in Plymouth, as I exclaimed 'I didn't have a clue where it was'.

When we got there the tour manager told us to go forth and multiply!

I have a ticket with 'guest' stamped on it some where in my artic that the Plymouth DJ Andy Howard gave me."

Chris Mannell (Plymouth, Devon)

Bon Jovi @ Cornwall Coliseum
October 2nd 1984

Break Out
Come Back
Roulette
Shot Through The Heart
Get Ready
Runaway

"The thing I remember most about the night was how good Bon Jovi were and how average Kiss were!
I bought a sleeveless tour t-shirt that night and then after the gig many of us went to the free HM (Heavy Metal) disco next door in the nightclub.
All told it was a great night and one of dozens I enjoyed there!!"
Paul Marsh (St Austell)

"Took coffee into Tina Turners dressing room on a boiling hot sunny day, Tina sat there in the biggest fur coat I had ever seen!"
Jane Hurley (ex- Cornwall Coliseum staff)

"Tina Turner was brilliant. I often wondered what happened to that signed autographed photo that was in the bar by the main entrance?"
K.N. Nankivell (Bodmin, Cornwall)

Whitesnake @ Cornwall Coliseum
March 6th 1984
Gambler

Guilty of Love

Ready An' Willing

Love Ain't No Stranger

Here I Go Again

Slow An' Easy

Crying In The Rain

Ain't No Love In the Heart of the City

Fool For Your Loving

Thank You Blues

Slide It In

Don't Break My Heart Again

"Two years later Whitesnake hit the Coliseum with their 'Slide It In' tour, with new guitarist John Sykes.
The support act was Great White followed by Whitesnake, playing new album material and many of their classics from previous albums.
Vocally lead singer David Coverdale has got to be up there as one of the best vocalists in rock and he proved that on the night."
Mark Jewitt (Plymouth, Devon)

"I could hardly contain my excitement as we travelled through the Styx towards Carlyon Bay near St. Austell. The trip from Plymouth seemed to take an age – especially when confined in my mums old Austin Allegro. It was 1984. This was the year I watched my first 'Heavy Metal' concert at the Cornwall Coliseum. I was just fifteen years old.
I was part of the crowd in June 1984 who watched Whitesnake perform on their 'Slide it in Tour' supported by Great White."
David J.B. Smith (Military Author – Plymouth)

"It was initially supposed to be just 'another gig' at the Coliseum, Saxon on the 'World Crusade Tour' but for me it was a lot worse than that –I had rampant food poisoning!

I hadn't drank ANY alcohol that day at all and on the way down on the coach I sat at the back and I remember throwing up all over the canvas covered floor.

Then I was sick in my hand and had to hold my other hand up to the driver when he came to collect the coach tickets.

On arrival at the venue I went in and still feeling ill spent a little while on the toilet, missing the support act and feeling worse for wear. I think then I may have bought a drink of coke or lemonade to make me feel better, but nothing seemed to work and I felt so hot; I was burning up with a fever.

I remember Saxon coming on and all I could think of was trying to cool, so I went to the back of the venue and lay on the 'disabled platform' with my face on the floor, relishing in the freezing cold canvas. People must have thought I was severely disabled or completely leathered, but no one moved me, no one spoke to me, which was a relief as I felt so poorly.

This was the 2nd time that I had seen Saxon at the Coliseum, but this time I missed most of the show and was pleased to get home, so not the usual visit!"

Ian Carroll (Author)

New Order @ Cornwall Coliseum
23rd August 1984

The Perfect Kiss
Ceremony
Ultraviolence
Sooner Than You Think
Your Silent Face
Thieves Like Us
5 8 6
Temptation

Blue Monday
Sunrise
Face Up

"I worked in the Wimpy summer of 1984 and then on breaks from University in 1985 and 1987. I was employed as a dishwasher initially, at the time Lisa Bulford was my girlfriend and her mum Heather ran the Wimpy. I quickly moved on to become a chef.
Best memories: all the time spent in the takeaway section with Toby Harris doing George and Zippy, pretending to go downstairs behind the counter and eating lunch with the two Heathers (Bulford and Wenmouth) as they discussed and dissected the young ladies who worked in the Wimpy.
Best working day was always Radio 1 Roadshow, in at about 7.00a.m and finishing about midnight after the roadshow disco.
The other bonus was getting to watch 15 minutes of every show on show nights."

Mark Roberts (Histon Nr Cambridge)

"When the shows were not sold out we were asked if we wanted free seats, one of these shows was Tina Turner. It was a great show."

Sheila Gill (Usherette – St Austell, Cornwall)

Iron Maiden @ Cornwall Coliseum
September 22nd 1984

Aces High
2 Minutes To Midnight
The Trooper
Revelations
Die With Your Boots On
Flight of Icarus
Rime of the Ancient Marina
Losfer Words (Big 'Orra)
Powerslave
The Number of the Beast
Hallowed Be Thy Name
22 Acacia Avenue
Iron Maiden
Run To The Hills
Running Free
Sanctuary

"1984. Iron Maiden on the back of a Harley Davidson. What self-respecting 13 year old wouldn't be drawn irrevocably into the world of live music with an introduction like that? These were my formative years of musical discovery and Maiden's galloping heavy metal had made the biggest impression on me so far. So naturally, when offered the chance to take a trip from Plymouth to Cornwall on the back of my sister's boyfriends' Harley D, with a convoy of other bikers, I was rather excitable. From memory, my Mother was less enamoured with the idea...the thermal long johns

she insisted I wear under my jeans weren't the most terribly metal of things but small sacrifices had to me made!

My memories of the trip down are a whirlwind of long hair, beards, denims, tobacco, patchouli oil and terrifyingly old bikers (in retrospect none of whom were probably past their early twenties but at 13 everybody seems ancient!). Stopping off in pubs, annoying the locals by putting '2 Minutes to Midnight' on the jukebox, a brief detour so that one of them could fulfil his lifetime ambition of urinating off of Lands' End (odd the things which stick in your mind...), it was all a rude but enlightening awakening to this naive and somewhat introverted young whippersnapper.

The gig itself, my first taste of live music (I'm not counting that Tommy Steele musical I got dragged to as a kid!), was a thrilling experience. The support band was called Waysted and I have little memories of them aside from a poodle-permed vocalist in ridiculously tight spandex. It was Maiden I was there for and they left me wide-eyed and pummelled ear in wonder, performing in front of their spectacular Egyptian styled stage. The set list has since gone down in Maiden folklore, being the same as presented on the legendary 'Live After Death' album released the following year.

A couple of other little things stick in the mind, one of the chaps I'd travelled down with voicing his exasperation when vocalist Bruce Dickinson introduced a new 13 minute song – 'Rime of the Ancient Mariner' - '13 bloody minutes?! How am I supposed to headbang for that long?!' and a brief moment of trouble when some ne'er do wells had kicked off towards the front of the crowd (I vaguely recall a knife being involved here, I distinctly recall Dickinson calling them out and telling them, in no uncertain terms, to go away). Fortunately, such moments have proven to be few and far between in the hundreds of rock and metal gigs I've subsequently attended (and from memory this turned out to be a rogue element who weren't fans anyway but had gone looking to stir the hornet's nest). Beyond that it was the crowd, the atmosphere, the volume, and the spectacle...indeed the entire experience made a lasting impression on me. If I wasn't already in love with music this cemented it and, although it would be two years before my next live gig (Maiden at the Cornwall Coliseum again!) by the age of 16 I was happily traipsing up to London as often as my finances would allow to see the likes of Slayer, Anthrax and Nuclear Assault.

The return journey is all but lost to memory. It was bloody cold, I remember that much, and that I was fair knackered when I got back. Maiden were popular in school at the time so I had a badge of honour to wear the following Monday...and that subsequent trip to see them in 1986 was with a coach full of school friends to witness Maiden being brilliant all over again. I'd never re-visit the Coliseum after that but for those two introductory gigs it'll always hold a special place in my heart."

Ian Salsbury (Plymouth, Devon)

"The only memory I have of the Coliseum is travelling down by coach to see Iron Maiden.
I remember necking a few cans on the way down, think I was quite pissed before the gig even started. I do remember the gig being a massive event for me; I mean its not every day you get to see the Maiden is it?
My biggest memory of the night, which is a bit sad really, was having to go outside and throw up. I hardly ever get that drunk, so I know I must have been completely hammered!"

Martin Northcott (Plymouth, Devon)

"I only went to the metal/rock gigs down the Coliseum and I have to say the first one was Iron Maiden on the 'Powerslave' tour, '84 I think it was.
As I had never been in there before I was that excited at seeing my favourite band for the first time in this (as I remember) massive venue with a full stage show I was sure I was going to pee myself, happily I didn't...
I went to a handful of great gigs after that.
I always felt that same buzz as I walked into the venue. Happy days."

Dave Oldham (Par, Cornwall)

"It was 22 September 1984 and I was again heading back to the Coliseum to watch a band who still define British Heavy Metal today. I have distinct memories of the Iron Maiden 'World Slavery Tour'.
Again my old mum drove me down to that concert. Years later she told me that a Coliseum doorman had said she could stand at the back - just to see what all the fuss was about.
Its not everyday one of your rock idols talks to you. Prior to Iron Maiden taking the stage I managed to get around the back of the Coliseum. At this time, Portacabins were situated at the rear and used as changing rooms for bands. I was standing away from the gathered throng of groupies and near an open Portacabin window.

Suddenly, looming into view was Bruce Dickinson. He saw me, smiled and was about to talk to me. Stupidly, because I was so excited, I shouted 'Its Bruce'. The shocked lead singer of Iron Maiden was mobbed by a crowd of equally excited teenagers. Bruce looked at me and said in his best, Lord Iffy Boatrace voice, 'Fek Awaff'."

David J.B. Smith (Military Author – Plymouth)

"At the time they were incredibly popular and had been quite credible for the early part of their career. UB40 were now evolving their Birmingham mixed race reggae sounds into a bona fide pop act and they were massive with their cover of Neil Diamond's 'Red Red Wine', which had been a number 1 on the UK charts in August the previous year.
Still liking them a lot, I made the hour long journey down from Plymouth and joined the sold out crowd – I even bought a wooly scarf, which I wore with my leather jacket, mixing rock and reggae styles together and I didn't care!!"

Ian Carroll (Author)

"Saw Paul Young twice – 1st time me & my friend bunked off college, got a bus down to the beach & waited by the entrance to be first in line to get in. Got there about 9.30am. Just after midday a security guard came out & asked if we needed some water or the loo. We asked if we could come inside & meet Paul. He laughed & went back in.
About half an hour later a bunch of coliseum staff came out to the car park & started a game of football. The same security chap came out & we asked again if we could go inside. He told us he didn't think we were very big fans of Paul. We said "of course we are – we wouldn't be here so early if we weren't". He asked whether we would actually recognise him if we saw him close up. We said, "of course we would!" He then told us that Paul & his band had walked straight past us & were now playing football behind us. (They weren't staff)
It didn't take us long to run to the car park & being 16 & a bit silly I went up to Paul & said "Are you Paul Young?" – what an idiot. Anyway it turned out okay because we got photos & autographs & even had a kick around with them until they went in when more people started arriving. I was doubly chuffed when Paul threw his towel into the audience at the end of the concert & I caught it. I still

have   it   to   this   day.
(Dawn, Somerset)

Depeche Mode @ Cornwall Coliseum
September 27th 1984
Something to Do
Two Minute Warning
Puppets
If You Want
People Are People
Leave In Silence
New Life
Shame
Somebody
Ice Machine
Lie to Me
Blasphemous Rumours
Told You So
Master and Servant
Photographic
Everything Counts
See You
Shout
Just Can't Get Enough

"Definitely remember Depeche Mode and the Some Great Reward tour.
David Gahan in black leather trousers and a blue flouncy silk

shirt...they were absolutely amazing!"
Jane Fitzwalter (Bodmin, Cornwall)

"Dio did a show that was full of heavy metal/hard rock antics and aggression...the full scary bad boy act.
RJD came off side stage and in an extremely modest demeanor and with a soft and eloquent voice asked..."was the show ok?"
He was quite nervous and 'shy'. A totally unexpected contrast.
The perfect gentleman to chat to after the show."
Clive Rodell (Sydney, Australia)

"On the 'Holy Diver Tour' I watched Dio supported by Queensryche.
It was 15 Sept 1984. I vividly remember the crowd surging forward and crushing me hard into the metal barrier. I must have looked a bit distressed. Reaching down from the stage, Ronnie James Dio passed me a plastic cup full of ice cool water. He was a real gentleman."
David J.B. Smith (Military Author – Plymouth)

Status Quo @ Cornwall Coliseum
July 7th 1984

Caroline
Paper Plane
Roll Over Lay Down
Backwater
Just Take Me
Little Lady
Don't Drive My Car
Whatever You Want

Mystery Song – Railroad – Most of the Time – Wild Side of Life – Again and Again – Slow Train (Medley)
Hold You Back
Rockin' All Over The World
Over The Edge
Dirty Water
Forty-Five Hundred Times
Big Fat Mama
Don't Waste My Time
Roadhouse Blues
What Your'e Proposing
Rain
Down Down
Bye Bye Johnny

"Hard to pick any one favourite gig – as a mad but ageing Status Quo fan (52 gigs to date) I would have to say that perhaps July 6th and 7th 1984 were special ones, the 'End Of The Road' tour, when I did both gigs at the Coliseum. To see Quo for what was supposed to be the last time was emotional for many to say the least. But here were are today and they are still rocking!"
Derek Hore (Paignton, Devon)

"Growing up in my teen years, the place came into my life once again when I would go and see my favourite bands, Hawkwind, Black Sabbath, Whitesnake, Rainbow, Motorhead and Status Quo. The last time I visited there was for Status Quo's 'End of the Road' tour in 1984. Shortly after our family moved from Cornwall and I didn't return until it was all closed down.
The Coliseum was a magical place for many different reasons but hopefully it will live on in people's memories. Long live the

Cornwall Coliseum!!"
Iain Armstrong (Whitstone, North Cornwall)

"I remember my dad taking me to see Orville sometime in the 80's I must have been around 4 maybe 5.
I still remember Orville coming on stage in a little white car and announcing he used 'Duckhams Oil'. Also my dad lifting me up so I could stroke Orville's tummy at the end. He was my first love!"
Claire Joanne Lee (St Austell, Cornwall)

"A highlight for me was Bo Diddley - a seldom mentioned gig, but an incredible night, the place was half empty, and I got to shake his hand!"
Mike Bennett (Cornwall)

The Smiths @ Cornwall Coliseum
June 22nd 1984

Nowhere Fast
Girl Afraid
Handsome Devil
This Charming Man
William, It Was Really Nothing
Heaven Knows I'm Miserable Now
Still Ill
I Don't Owe You Anything
Jeane
Barbarism Begins At Home
Hand In Glove
Pretty Girls Make Graves
Miserable Lie
What Difference Does It Make?
You've Got Everything Now

"Went to my very first concert 'The Smiths' at the Coliseum when I was 15 with my best friend Lindsey. How grown up we felt – the gig was awesome!! Also saw The Mission there several years later - another happy memory care of the Coliseum."
Natalie Hobman (Callington, Cornwall)

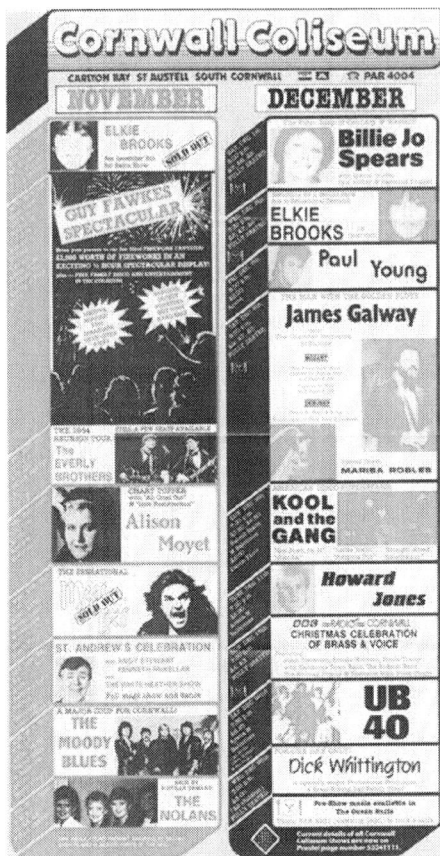

"I went to many metal gigs at the Coliseum (Maiden, Motorhead, Lizzy, Saxon) and remember walking that road from Holmbush down to the Coliseum several times.
After the Saxon gig in Feb '84 my mate and I (both aged 15) had a prearranged lift organised to Liskeard - it was my Mum's friend and her chap - Chris.
Anyway, after the gig, we queued at the front entrance - as the band had promised to do a signing session. As we stood and waited the car park emptied and the more it cleared, the more agitated my pal (Adam) became! He was almost in tears when only a handful of cars remained in the main car park.
The more he urged me to abandon the cause and get our lift, the more I told him to 'eff off 'We can get home whatever happens, but I might not get an opportunity to meet Saxon again - f#ck off - you

can go, but I ain't going anywhere!!' I could see Chris & Yvonne waiting patiently in their car for us and eventually our 'taxi' departed - and I later discovered that they were none too pleased!! That was it - Adam was distraught and I could only repeat that we would deal with our travel problems once we get our gear signed (priorities, right?). Anyway, after a long wait, we had our tour books signed (still have mine) and I was so chuffed, I'd have happily walked the 26 miles home. No need though, I 'phoned Mum at some unholy hour and declared that we were stranded - Chris hadn't turned up...

We were collected a little later and Chris received a rollicking for his troubles - Ha ha. It was several years later when I actually confessed and apolgised and luckily enough I didn't receive a clip around the ear either.

I met 'Nibbs' a few years ago when Saxon supported Motorhead and relayed that tale to him - he pissed himself. I also got a gig poster signed by the band, so that'll rub salt into Chris' wounds - sorry fella!!"

Mark Shaw (Liskeard, Cornwall)

"I have such happy memories of Cornwall Coliseum, and having the pleasure of seeing some of the top artists and bands in the world; including the Police, Genesis, Chas & Dave and my idol Buddy Rich and meeting them back-stage, and getting an auto-graph or pic with them was a dream come true!! Also remember Quasar's/Gossip's and Roller-Skating in arena!"

Nigel Balsdon(Bodmin, Cornwall)

Meat Loaf @ Cornwall Coliseum
21st November 1984

Bad Attitude
Dead Ringer For Love
Jumpin' the Gun
Midnight at the Lost and Found
I'm Gonna Love Her for Both of Us
Paradise by the Dashboard Light
Nowhere Fast

Piece of the Action
All Revved Up With No Place to Go
Modern Girl
Two Out of Three Ain't Bad
Bad Out of Hell

"My final memory of the Coliseum was seeing Meatloaf on his 'Bad Attitude' tour playing old and new classics.
Meatloaf celebrated his birthday on the night and was presented with a birthday cake on stage with a rendition of 'Happy Birthday' from the Coliseum crowd."
Mark Jewitt (Plymouth, Devon)

"My husband watched Dr Hook there in 1984."
Patricia Darch (St Austell, Cornwall)

1985

*T*his year musically was dominated by 'Live Aid' at Wembley Stadium (and I was lucky enough to be there) and at JFK Stadium in Philadelphia. At 12 O'clock GMT Status Quo kicked off the event with 'Rocking All Over The World' the most suitable song for the most appropriate time. Queen secured themselves as the most amazing stadium band of the time and U2 stepped up a level, all thanks to Bono grabbing a girl out of the crowd and making a memorable TV moment.

In the cinemas 'Back to the Future' was released and became one of the biggest and most popular films of the year and kickstarted the successful trilogy.

The beginning of the phasing out of the UK's red telephone boxes began,'Neighbours' debuted in Australia, 'Amadeus' won the Best Movie Oscar, the 'Discovery Channel' launched, Ricky Nelson died in a plane crash, the first Nintendo Home Games system launched in the USA and the Brixton Riots took place.

The best selling single of the year in the UK was 'The Power of Love' by Jennifer Rush and the Christmas single came from the man in 'double denim' - 'Merry Christmas Everyone' by Shakin' Stevens.

"I'm sorry but I have no real memories of the venue apart from it being big and cold when I was there, the reception I do remember was great."
Fish (Marillion – Vocals)

Marillion @ Cornwall Coliseum

December 14th 1985

Emerald Lies
Script For A Jesters Tear
Incubus
Chelsea Monday
The Web
Pseudo Silk Kimono
Kayleigh
Lavender
Bitter Suite
Heart of Lothian
Waterhole (Expresso Bongo)
Lords of the Backstage
Blind Curve
Childhood's End?
White Feather
Fugazi
Garden Party
Market Square Heroes

"Fish era Marillion were amazing. When I saw Marillion at the Coliseum in December '85 it was the fifth chance that I had to see them in a quite short period of time and they were one of my favourites.
I had seen them in the summer at Monsters of Rock at Donington, where they didn't really fit in, but in Cornwall in front of 'their' fans they could do no wrong. I went there with Kevin, Andy, Martin,

Tony and Kathy and we all had a great time, drinking, laughing and singing along; Kevin was yet again the driver, but he didn't mind and I think that this might have been the time that Tony had to travel in the boot as we didn't have enough room in the car."

Ian Carroll (Author)

"I worked in the Wimpy from 1985 to 1988 and had a ball.
Although I didn't particularly like selling ice creams in the intervals of the concerts we did get to see part of the act, which was great!
I remember serving Terence Trent D'Arby who wrote on my order

pad ' To Jo a Wimpy Bean burger'!"
Jo Tubb (St Austell, Cornwall)

"In the time before mobile phones and digital camera how we had to try to stop the audience taking photographs of different acts. Sometimes bags were searched before the audience was seated but even when this happened many devices got through. We spent much of the evening pointing out torches at the offending people to no avail because the minute you turned your back they started again.
The funniest thing was that they always took the pictures of their favourite songs and they probably got blurred images."
Sheila Gill (Usherette – St Austell, Cornwall)

The Damned @ Cornwall Coliseum
29th June 1985
Curtain Call
Shadow of Love
Neat Neat Neat
Wait for the Blackout
Grimly Fiendish
Stranger on the Town
Is It a Dream
There'll Come a Day
Smash It Up
I Had Too Much to Dream –
(Last Night)
Looking At You
Gun Fury (of Riot Forces)
Street Of Dreams
Curtain Call (Reprise)
Lust For Life
Love Song
New Rose

Disco Man
Born to Kill

Cornwall Coliseum
CARLYON BAY, ST AUSTELL, SOUTH CORNWALL — ☎ PAR 4004

THURSDAY 31st October 8 p.m. £4.23	PLYMOUTH SOUND PRESENTS THE BEST OF BRITISH COUNTRY WITH **RAYMOND FROGGATT AND ROSE-MARIE** WITH KELVIN HENDERSON, MALCOLM ANTONY AND THE YELLOWSTONE PICNIC BAND	SATURDAY 23rd November & SUNDAY 24th November 7.30 p.m. £12.50 Balcony £11.00 Arena **ELTON JOHN**
FRIDAY 1st November 8 p.m. £5	DON'T WATCH THAT, WATCH THIS **MADNESS** THE MAD/NOT MAD TOUR	SATURDAY 30th November 6.30 p.m. & 9.30 p.m. £10, £8 BACK BY OVERWHELMING DEMAND THE **EVERLY BROTHERS**
TUESDAY 5th November 7.30 p.m. £5	**LEVEL 42** NEW SINGLE 'SOMETHING ABOUT YOU'	SATURDAY 7th December 7.30 p.m. £4.50 **BLANCMANGE**
SATURDAY 9th November 8 p.m. £5.50	**SIOUXSIE AND THE BANSHEES** WITH SPECIAL GUESTS THE SCIENTISTS	THURSDAY 12th December 7.30 p.m. £5 **ECHO AND THE BUNNYMEN** NEW SINGLE 'BRING ON THE EMPTY HORSES'
WEDNESDAY 13th November 7.30 p.m. £6, £5	**GO WEST**	SATURDAY 14th December 8 p.m. £6.50 **MARILLION**
FRIDAY 15th November 8 p.m. £5	**KING** 'ALONE WITHOUT YOU'	SUNDAY 15th December 7.30 p.m. £4, £3 RADIO CORNWALL'S CHRISTMAS CELEBRATION of BRASS & VOICE
MONDAY 18th November 7.30 p.m. £8.£7	**SADE** SOLD OUT 'YOUR LOVE IS KING' & 'SMOOTH CREATOR'	MONDAY 23rd December 7.30 p.m. £6 LEGENDARY GUITAR HERO **NILS LOFGREN** CRY TOUGH
FRIDAY 22nd November 8 p.m. £5 Table Seating	ST ANDREW'S CELEBRATION WITH **ANDY STEWART AND ISLA ST CLAIR** AND THE WHITE HEATHER DANCERS	SATURDAY 22nd February 8 p.m. £5 **OMD** 'CRUSH TOUR' PLEASE NOTE THIS DATE HAS BEEN RESCHEDULED

"*I came back from London on the day that I went to see Elton John and I remember getting in quite late in the afternoon and having to go straight to the coach station from home. My friend Andy Harris was at the door talking to my father when I arrived and I always remember him saying that my dad looked liked Val Doonican - he looked nothing like him to be honest, but it was dark.*

The coach journey down took a long time as there were traffic jams on the way, it seemed that half of Devon and a Cornwall were on their way to the Coliseum that night; we went to see him on the Sunday night *which was his second night there, I'm sure that the previous nights traffic was just as chaotic.*

When we arrived at the Coliseum and the coach started to make its way down the steep hill, a man was let onboard the coach, by the driver, selling 'fake' programs, thirty seconds or so later a security guard got on, confiscated the programs and removed the chancer from the bus. The security guard then passed out all the programs for free, I got one, but after looking at it and how cheap it was, I was glad that I didn't pay!!!

Elton's show that night was brilliant, a greatest hits set and he had plenty to choose from. I've seen him several times since including recently at the Eden Sessions this year at the Eden Project, but no show could've been better than at the Coliseum that cold night in November. The intimacy of the venue, the closeness of the bar - where if you positioned yourself right you could still watch the band through an open door as you waited to get served, you couldn't beat it for a venue."

Ian Carroll (Author, Plymouth)

"Elton John who was agitated early into his performance that the sound wasn't right but also carried on singing whilst furiously gesturing for a sound engineer to fix the sound issue."

Lee Slaughter (St Austell)

"I remember Elton John picking up his piano stool and throwing it across the stage and the whole crowd was amazed."

Clive Green (St Day, Cornwall)

"Paul Young accidentally hit a female fan at the front of the crowd as he swung his microphone with full length stand from side to side whilst singing.

He carried on singing for a few minutes as he comforted her whilst kneeling at the front of the stage!"

Lee Slaughter (St Austell)

"The summer I worked on the beach has many memories. Probably the most dramatic of these involved rescuing a swimmer who was in trouble and bringing him back to the main area of the beach to a waiting ambulance.

It all happened on a rather dull day the beach was very quiet however we had set the beach up as normal and had the rescue boat   ready   to   launch.

We got a message that there was a swimmer in trouble off Polgaver Beach. We launched the rescue boat and I went at full *speed the length of the beach and then headed out to where he had been seen. I managed to locate him in the water he was wearing jeans and was really struggling. I managed to pull him into the boat and then headed back to Polgaver to pick up the lifeguard from there to look after him as he was barely conscious. I picked him up and headed back to the main part of the beach again as fast as we could go. On reaching the main area I drove the boat straight up the beach and he was taken to the waiting ambulance. I later found out that he had stopped breathing but the ambulance crew had resuscitated him. Following this I received personal letter of thanks from Graham McNally and free tickets to a show of my choice."* **Andy Gill (Coliseum Staff, St Austell, Cornwall)**

"My all time favourite was Paul Young, the week before Live Aid where he sang a song with Alison Moyet. They practiced the song during his concert and it was great. Paul Young is, of all the artists I've seen, the only one who genuinely sounded the same as if listening to them on a CD." **Kevin Bentley (Plymouth, Devon)**

"Victoria Wood did a brilliant show and kept the audience entertained all evening and I remember her show especially because she was one of the only performers to say thank you directly to us." **Sheila Gill (Usherette – St Austell, Cornwall)**

"2nd Paul Young concert was in summer and the beach was busy so he didn't leave the building but his band & backing singers did – got some photos & autographs with them.
WE were at the front again & saw a girl we both recognised from the last concert. She had been standing at the front but on the other side to us during the 1st concert & when Paul swung his microphone around it hit her on the head & she was taken away unconscious.
I believe she got flowers or something as an apology. Anyway we spot this girl & she's standing there with her hands on her head! As soon as Paul comes on stage she starts wailing "Mind my head Paul, Mind my head" She kept this up all the first half until someone told her to shut up or she'd have more than her head to worry about!" **Dawn (Somerset)**

"Another memory pops up. A dinner dance in the Ocean Suite, where, with a girlfriend, we decided we were a bit hot and went for a swim in the pool; which was actually visible to the whole of the dining room. Oops."

Jenny Parnwell (Fowey, Cornwall)

"I seemed to live here during the 80s!
First gig was Duran Duran - but also saw Toyah, Howard Jones, ABC, Nils Lofgren and others!
Radio One Road Show every year round the back and roller disco on Sunday afternoons!
Watched Hurricane Higgins play a show match against Dennis Taylor there. Played Boothill in the arcade before going to Wimpy for a Coke Float!
Had Tech Dance at The Ocean Suite, went to baby Bentleys, Bentleys and then Quasars ('..be seen there!) Funk-a-Duck disco in the main hall and beach in the summer!
Used to go up that hill in my 2CV in first gear, roof down with mates standing up with their arms waving out the top of the car!!
Happy days!"

Alison Hague (Par, Cornwall)

The Cure @ Cornwall Coliseum
8th September 1985

The Baby Screams
Play For Today
Kyoto Song
Primary
The Hanging Garden
Cold
In Between Days

Screw
A Night Like This
Let's Go to Bed
The Walk
Push
One Hundred Years
A Forest
Sinking
Close To Me
Charlotte Sometimes
At Night
Boys Don't Cry
Three Imaginary Boys
10:15 Saturday Night
Killing an Arab
Forever

"Then in 1985 my mum found me a job at weekends and holidays-cleaning at the coliseum!! (How lucky was I? Not!).
My friend Yvonne Kelly called for me each morning and we cycled down - fortunately the kind other ladies protected us from the delights of the men's loos!
Through my student days I progressed, first to ice cream selling and then to work behind the bar.
In my time behind the bar I experienced watching some of many bands, including T'Pau, The Stranglers, Engelbert Humperdink and the Flying Pickets - who came and drank in the bar afterwards. I went to see Level 42 and Paul Young - for the Paul Young concert I was right at the front of the stage: those were the days of no seating throughout a concert."
Alison Pearson (Nr Exeter, Devon)

1986

Two Terrible disasters dominated the news this year, the first was the Challenger Space Shuttle exploding only 73 seconds into its launch killing all seven astronauts and the nuclear accident at Chernobyl in Ukraine, 31 deaths were attributed directly to the accident, but thousand more were to die from cancer related illnesses.

'Out Of Africa' won the Best Film Oscar, 'Short Circuit' was released, Diego Maradona performed the 'Hand Of God' goal to knock England out of the World Cup in Mexico – with Argentina going on to win the tournament, in London Prince Andrew married Sarah Ferguson, the 'Oprah Winfrey' show debuted, the M25 opened and Mike Tyson won his first world boxing title against Trevor Berbick in Las Vegas.

It was a very busy year in the world of movies with Gemma Atterton, Jamie Bell of 'Billy Elliot' fame, Robert Pattinson of the 'Twilight' series, Shia LaBeouf and Lindsay Lohan all being born and in Manhattan, Stefani Joanne Angelina Germanotta was born, who 22 years later was to go on to dominate and rule the pop world as Lady Gaga. The music and movie worlds lost Phil Lynott of Thin Lizzy, James Cagney and Cary Grant.

The best selling single of the year in the UK was 'Don't Leave Me This Way' The Communards and the Christmas number one was 'Reet Petite' by Jackie Wilson, accompanied by a wonderful 'claymation' video.

"I remember how nervous we all were so long ago performing at the Coliseum in the eighties.
The audience was electric, and all we could hear was the

wonderful anticipation from the crowd as they chanted 'Five Star' to what seemed like a thousand times.
I know there was never a time that I was ever ready to go out and face a crowd without my stomach full of butterflies, my brothers and sisters would probably say the same. In saying that, we have wonderful memories from that show, some of our most memorable and it is always so much fun watching it back and seeing how strange, wonderful and young we looked back then.
Great fun!"
Lorraine Pearson (Five Star – Vocals)

"Ahem…
Unfortunately I have no memory or stories of this moment!"
Tony James (Sigue Sigue Sputnik – Guitar)

"I know I played there – but apart from remembering it's wonderful sea-shore setting – and how far from London it was --- I have no recollections at all!"
Tom McGuinness (The Blues Band – Guitar)

The Smiths @ Cornwall Coliseum
17th October 1986

The Queen Is Dead
Panic
I Want the One I Can't Have
Vicar in a Tutu
There is a Light That Never Goes –Out
Ask
Rusholme Ruffians
Frankly, Mr Shankly

The Boy With the Thorn in His Side
What She Said
Is It Really So Strange?
Never had No One Ever
Cemetry Gates
London
Meat Is Murder
I Know It's Over
The Draize Train
How Soon Is Now?
Still Ill
Bigmouth Strikes Again

"Getting drunk was usually the name of the game when we went to a gig at the Coliseum. I remember drinking all the way down in the car, then going to a pub and finally shopping in Leo's in St Austell and walking around the supermarket with a large shopping trolley and buying just a pork pie – we thought we were very funny, we were actually very annoying and very drunk.

At the time I had very long hair, died black and thought I was the proverbial 'bees knees' in my fringed suede jacket and cowboy boots, which were all very popular at the time.

We arrived at the Coliseum, parked up in the already busy car park, each of us very pissed except for the designated driver Kev (who was the only one of us who actually drove – God rest his soul) and went to have a play on the beach. We threw stones in the sea, kicked pebbles on the beach and fell over several times due to the level of alcohol in our blood.

Being May it wasn't too cold, not that we would have been able to notice anyway, being so drunk.

When we went into the venue the support band Beltane Fire went past in a blur and then it was time for the Ramones.

They played like they always did – fast and furious.

Every song started with a quick '1,2,3,4' and within just over an hour and 35 songs or so, it was all over.

My friend Lee fainted at one point during the show, but because the crowd was so tightly packed he didn't collapse onto the ground, we were near the front you see and we were squished together like sardines in a rock 'n' roll tin.

All in all, an excellent time and another legendary band, playing at 'our venue'.

Ian Carroll (Author, Plymouth)

"I saw the Ramones down there as well about and the only thing Joey Ramone said all the way through the set was '1,2,3,4' that joined every song being played at break neck speed ...frantic gig that one..."

Kevan Ball (Plymouth)

"Mid 80's went to the Coliseum to see the mighty Ramones.

After hearing that some mates got to the venue early for a previous Damned gig and met and played pinball with the band, we decided to see if we could do the same with Da Bruddas.

Getting there about 5'ish we wandered around the site to see if we could locate any of them but no joy. Thought we would try and sneak around the back to see if we would have better luck there.

On walking past the front entrance we passed two obvious Ramones fans wearing all the gear (leather jackets and ripped jeans) going the other way. We just nodded and walked on. One had a Ramones haircut but the other had a more Punky Spiky hairstyle. Anyway no joy around the back so we just carried on and went to the gig.

The Ramones came on stage and we realised we had walked past Johnny Ramone and Dee Dee Ramone (now sporting a spiky haircut). Doh!

They were magnificent though (Too Tough To Die tour I think)."

Rick Matthews (Falmouth, Cornwall)

"I visited the Cornwall Coliseum on a number of occasions but the one that sticks out in my mind the most is the Ramones gig I think around 1986.

After a couple of pub stops I vaguely remember visiting a supermarket where the author of this book bought a solitary pork pie and used a shopping trolley to transport it round the store.

There was also a crisp packet incident in one of the pubs where *one of us popped a crisp packet and some geezer had a go at us complaining of a heart condition.*

This was followed by frolicking on the beach by which time we were all pretty much hammered.

Can't remember much of the gig itself sadly other than it was at break neck speed with only the solitary cry of "1, 2, 3, 4" splitting one song from another.... happy daze."

Andy Harris (Plymouth, Devon)

"Alison Moyet had shot some of her video there and I remember seeing it on the telly."

Andy Boddington (Plymouth, Devon)

"Once the seating was put in, took my children to see Showaddywaddy. And also went with a group of girls to see the Chippendales. Carefully chose seats away from the front that time."

Jenny Parnwell (Fowey, Cornwall)

"My favourite memory of the Coliseum has to be the fantastic Shirley Bassey concert. I have been to other venues to see Shirl

but the Coliseum had a sort of intimate atmosphere. Best ever."
Anne Williams (St Columb Major, Cornwall)

"Whilst doing Security for the Chuck Berry gig at Cornwall Coliseum, two fans came forward to the stage barrier with a programme from a Chuck Berry concert 15 years earlier. They wanted to gain entry to meet Chuck Berry and get him to sign their programme.
We could not allow entry, however my fellow bouncer Ron said he would go backstage with the programme and get it signed. Ron returned a short while later, somewhat agitated. Chuck Berry had said, "Well if they have waited 15 years, they can wait another 15

years and told Ron to get out!!"
Clive Rodell (Sydney, Australia)

MONDAY 2ND JUNE
At 8.00 p.m.

A Living Legend

Chuck Berry

LIVE . . . .

Tickets In Advance £5.00

SATURDAY 7TH JUNE
At 8.00 p.m.

TOM ROBINSON
and SECTOR 27

£2.50

"I have been searching through my diaries to see what date it was that Chuck Berry was there. I think it was in the late 80s. I know it was when there was still roller-skating in the main hall, with a bar along the right hand side, looking at the stage. A few tables and chairs were dotted around, but mainly it was just people standing drinking or dancing, and it was not really very full.
I was dancing in the front. Love that music, 'can't sit still music'.
At one point Chuck Berry invited anyone wearing green to come on the stage and dance. (It was in the time when all in one overall

type things were fashionable. I had a green one with a zip up the front, which I used to leave rather low!)

So with about four others, I climbed onto the stage and boogied away. Chuck Berry beckoned to me to move along the stage closer to him. I chickened out because of his reputation, but I enjoyed the dancing.

PS I still have the green overalls.

PPS But they don't fit now."

Jenny Parnwell (Fowey, Cornwall)

Status Quo @ Cornwall Coliseum
December 19th 1986

Whatever You Want
Paper Plane
Roll Over Lay Down
Dreamin'
Little Lady
Mystery Song / Railroad / Most of the
Time / Wild Side of Life / Rollin' Home

/ Again and Again / Slow Train –
Medley
Hold You Back
Don't Drive My Car
Dirty Water
In The Army Now
Rockin' All Over The World
Big Fat Mama
Don't Waste My Time
Roadhouse Blues
Caroline
Rain
Down Down
Bye Bye Johnny

"STATUS QUO 'In The Army' tour!
December 1986 - I was 12yrs old, my sister 14yrs, mum and dad,
thankfully we were seated in the right balcony as you look at the
stage- was I a Quo fan?? I don't know but I spent most of the
concert watching the crowd below, at the age of 12 it was
fascinating watching heavy metal fans drinking beer and crowd
surfing!!
Although now I know that Status Quo aren't Heavy metal- back
then it was my first experience of Rock?
My sister doesn't remember even being there, and always denies
it! I pull her leg whenever there is any mention of Status Quo
telling people she is their number one fan! Lol"
Julie Smith (Plymouth, Devon)

"This was the first time I had seen Quo since they supported
Queen   on   the   'Magic   Tour'.
With the new line up, they didn`t disappoint, starting off with some
old classics.

Since I was just old enough to drink, going to what was the longest bar in Europe was fun, as they didn`t even bother asking for ID. Then it was a case of jumping aboard the Concert Travel Club coach back to Plymouth then a quick dash to the nightclub before they shut at 02:00."

John Lintern (Plymouth, Devon)

"We had a particularly harsh winter, not many passers by, and one night a group of lads knocked the door, long hair and denims. My parents were a bit concerned, but it turned out that they were serious Status Quo fans and some of the nicest young men you would ever wish to meet. They visited for several years to follow, with girlfriends, then wives. One of the nicer stories from life in a B & B."

Nancy (St Blazey, Cornwall)

"I also saw Status Quo and they were soo loud, I'm sure the damaged the foundation." **Kevin**

Bentley (Plymouth, Devon)

"The 1st 'Farewell Concert' there seemed to be about a 1000 since the last Quo concert I went to. I walked out before the end when they done the crap song 'In The Army Now'. I saw them 2-3 times before down there and they were good. I prefer to remember them in their hay day and not as the 'crap band' that played that drivel."

K.N. Nankivell (Bodmin, Cornwall)

"I'm 50 next month so all my memories of concerts at the Coliseum, Roller Disco, Quasars, The Ocean Suite and the 'Biggest Wimpy in the country' are all buried in tea-chests, shrouded by dust sheets, hidden in the archives in my brain!!"

Jeff Barrett (Spain)

"David Essex – I only went so I could hear 'Silver Dream Racer' live. I'm not really a fan, but the song would get into my top 500."

K.N. Nankivell (Bodmin, Cornwall)

"The Cornish Christmas Cracker concert was hosted by Radio Cornwall presenter Duncan Warren, it must have been 1980 something it was brass bands Cornish singers and if I remember rightly the late Al Hodge and his band."

Tracey Lander (Bodmin, Cornwall)

"I never did see a concert at the Coliseum, such a shame, although I would have probably been behind the pillar knowing my luck.
As I grew older we progressed to rollerskating in the main hall, I was never any good but it was always good music and a great atmosphere.
Quasars- Be seen there! This was my first night club experience (Baby Quazars) and I remember I had to have a Paisley shirt to fit in! Many a good night was had and this was later followed by Gossips, we all used to meet at 'Holmbush' pub and take a taxi down later. Half of St Austell met here and I am sure some are still together! In later years I was working in the warehouse of a large local supermarket on the by-pass, and on Friday nights we used to save our break until 11.45pm so that we could get ready to go to Gossips after work for two hours, most people had been drinking all night so we were always guaranteed a laugh at someone's expense.
The walk home always sobered me up, still to this day I cannot remember the number of steps from the bottom car park to the top car park or even how I got home in one piece!"
Richard Ruse (St Austell, Cornwall)

Cocteau Twins @ Cornwall Coliseum
14th November 1986

Lazy Calm
Hitherto
Sigh's Smell of Farewell
My Love paramour
Plain Tiger
Love's Easy Tears
My Hue and Cry
Sugar Hiccup

Pearly-Dewdrops' Drops
Pink Orange Red
Aikea-Guinea
Sea, Swallow Me

"I went to the Cornwall Coliseum for the 'Disco Against Drugs' concert. Members of the Grange Hill cast were the headliners, lots of schools from the Plymouth area took part."
Sara Ball (Plymouth, Devon)

Van Morrison @ Cornwall Coliseum 21st November 1986

Moondance
Celtic Swing
Northern Muse (Solid Ground)
Vanlose Stairway
It's All in the Game / Make it Real One
More Time
Help Me
Tir Na Nog
She Gives Me Religion
Cleaning Windows
A Sense of Wonder
And the Healing Has Begun
Dweller on the Threshold
Here Comes the Knight

In The Garden
Summertime in England
Full Force Gale
Bright Side of the Road
Rave On, John Donne
Grits Ain't Groceries

"Although we now live near Truro, we lived in Barnstaple from 1971 to 2006 and I used to drive down to Cornwall Coliseum during the 1980's to see:
Billy Connolly, Iron Maiden, Kiss, Dio, Bon Jovi, Queensryche, Bryan Adams, T'pau among others."
Les Deacon (Tresillian, Cornwall)

"I used to take my two young sons in the eighties to watch the big bonfires on the beach and the big firework displays on carnival night."
Patricia Darch (St Austell, Cornwall)

Ultravox @ Cornwall Coliseum
11th November 1986

Same Old Story
The Voice
New Europeans
Sweet Surrender
White China
Dream On
All in One Day
Time to Kill
All Stood Still
Hymn

Lament
Vienna
Passing Strangers
The Prize
One Small Day
Love's Great Adventure
Dancing With Tears in My Eyes
All Fall Down

"I remember going to see Ultravox with my friend Kev, as he was driving as usual. It was a brilliant night and I was very drunk, just for a change in my early twenty's and then afterwards we went into 'Quazars' (I think it was called that at the time) for a bit of a drink and seeing if anyone would dance with us, they didn't – sadly we left alone."
Ian Carroll (Author, Plymouth)

"This was the day before my birthday, not much else to say other than it was a really good electronic gig." **John Lintern (Plymouth, Devon)**

Cornwall Coliseum

CARLYON BAY ST.AUSTELL SOUTH CORNWALL ☎ PAR 4004

★ ★ ★ SEPTEMBER ★ ★ ★

Magnum

Nana Mouskouri

★ ★ ★ OCTOBER ★ ★ ★

The Bloodfire Posse
& The Christians

Someshow on Tour 86 '87

IRON MAIDEN

Joan Armatrading

The 2nd Restormel Prom
featuring
Restormel Concert Band
Cornwall Male Voice Choir
St Austell Amateur Operatic Society
Carclaze, Mount Charles & Bishop
Bennacoule Junior Schools
Fowey, St Stephens + Poltair Senior School
in aid of St Austell District Hospital
League of Friends

The Smiths

Klaus Wunderlich

Leo Sayer

★ ★ ★ NOVEMBER ★ ★ ★

Guy Fawkes Night Firework Display

Alison Moyet

HARPBEAT '86 PRESENTS

Ultravox

British Wildlife Appeal Film Show
introduced by Julian Pettifer

Sly and Robbie's Taxi Gang
plus
Yellowman + Half Pint
Ini Kamoze

★ ★ ★ DECEMBER ★ ★ ★

Billy Ocean

GoWest
plus special guest

BILLY CONNOLLY

Radio Cornwall Christmas Show
With Camborne Town Band
Mount Charles Band
Penzance Orpheus Ladies' Choir
Trevissue Male Voice Choir
Cornwall Concert Singers

HARPBEAT '86 presents

Status Quo

Extra Show Friday 19th December

The Stranglers

cornwall coliseum

ST. AUSTELL

1981-86 FIVE STAR YEARS
★ ★ ★ ★ ★

★ ★ ★ FEBRUARY ★ ★ ★

WEDNESDAY, 19th February 7.30 p.m. All Seats, £4	# JOHN MARTYN
SATURDAY, 22nd February 8 p.m. £5	# OMD 'CRUSH TOUR'

★ ★ ★ MARCH ★ ★ ★

SATURDAY, 8th March 7.30 p.m. £5, £4	DUTCHY OPERA PRESENTS **EXCELSIOR** A VICTORIAN EVENING WITH **BEN LUXON** **JOHN TRELEAVAN** AND **CHRIS BLOUNT** of BBC Radio Cornwall
SATURDAY, 29th March 2.30 p.m. £4, £3 £1 off kids	THE EASTER TREAT FOR ALL THE FAMILY **STU FRANCIS** & THE STARS OF **CRACKERJACK**

★ ★ ★ APRIL ★ ★ ★

FRIDAY, 4th April 8 p.m. £10, £8	**WEMBLEY COMES WEST** STARRING **GEORGE JONES** ★ **JANIE FRICKE** **JOHNNY RUSSEL** ★ **BILL MUNROE** THE GREATEST LINE UP OF AMERICAN COUNTRY STARS EVER SEEN IN THE WEST COUNTRY

1987

*I*n the world this year it was agreed that the construction of Disneyland Paris – later to become 'Euro Disney' – would begin, Aretha Franklin was the first woman to ever become inducted into the 'Rock And Rock Hall of Fame', Michael Jackson released 'BAD', U2 released their 'classic' album 'The Joshua Tree' that would see their star rise and them become international superstars and Margaret Thatcher saw her third term as Prime Minster of the UK begin.

On TV 'The Simpsons' appeared for the first time as a short cartoon interlude on the 'Tracy Ullman Show' and 'Star Trek Next Generation started broadcasting.

In world news Terry Waite was kidnapped in Beirut and the Zeebrugge Ferry disaster took place with the sinking of the Herald Of Free Enterprise, Nazi prisoner of war Rudolf Hess hung himself in his cell at the Spandau Prison in west Berlin and the Kings Cross Underground fire caused the deaths of 31 people and injured 100 more.

Many legendary characters passed away this year including Liberace, Andy Warhol, Fred Astaire, Lee Marvin and Maria Von Trapp who the movie 'The Sound of Music' was based on. People born this year include Maria Sharapova, Novak Djokovic, Lionel Messi, Zac Efron and Karen Gillan who starred as Amy Pond in Doctor Who from 2010-13 and went on to star as Nebula in the Marvel smash hit movie 'The Guardians of the Galaxy'.

The best selling single of the year in the UK was by the legendary Rick Astley with 'Never Gonna Give You Up' and the Christmas number one came from the Pet Shop Boys with 'Always On My Mind'.

"It is a tragedy when any theatre closes.
I did work a couple of times at the Coliseum.
I toured the 'Think of a Number Road Show', which was my One Man Educational Show from around 1980 to 1993. I then toured in 'Tales of Math's' and 'Legends' in 2000.
I may also have appeared there in daytime lectures for combined schools, which sort of rings a bell.
I always remember thinking it was strangely placed and out of the way - but that's about it."
Johnny Ball (Think Of A Number TV Show)

"I was an usherette at the Coliseum from 1987 until it closed. My name badge had "PAT USHERETTE" on it, which sometimes amused customers! Some actually did! Of course, they all thought they were the first ones to notice it."
Pat Naylor (Usherette Penzance, Cornwall)

"I was hugely into Roller-skating as a kid- influenced by Cliff Richard's single "Wired for Sound"- the video of Cliff on roller skates with a Walkman!!!
I was lucky enough to once attend one of the day time Roller Disco's there - true 80's memories."
Julie Smith (Plymouth, Devon)

"I worked at the Coliseum from 1987-1993. In 1987 I saw Terence Trent D'arby live, he was brilliant, (a kind of fusion of Prince and James Brown).

Gigs I saw snippets of whilst working were Bryan Adams, Status Quo, Marillion, Simply Red and numerous others. While working there I met Fish (Marillion), Jason Donovan and his backing singer Shelley Preston (previously of Bucks Fizz) who were rehearsing dance routines in the main hall.

I served Ted Rogers (3,2,1) a round of drinks in the Foyer Bar after a show and served Bruno Brooks (Radio One DJ) a drink who was a guest star at a Malibu promotional night in Quasars."

Richard Godfrey (St Austell, Cornwall)

"I remember seeing a lot of bands down at the Coliseum all different genres from a Cornish Christmas cracker with local brass bands etc. Magnum and Thin Lizzy to Terence Trent D'arby whose support act was Simply Red!

And the famous roller-skating sessions on a Sunday if we were lucky we would get to go to both the afternoon and evening sessions.

The Wimpy bar where everyone met up for chips at 30p per portion those were the days.

The nightclubs with their various names Bentleys, Quasars etc. Many a college Disco there with great music from DJ Butch.

I remember food exhibitions there in the main arena nothing else like it. Not to mention the arcade above the Wimpy playing pool there, waiting for skating to start.

I also remember club nights there when the arcade packed up

hard house and trance music lots of memories shared with school friends, family and college friends."
Tracey Lander (Bodmin, Cornwall)

"I can remember that during roller-skating watching people fall over with skates on whilst holding a pint of beer and spilling very little if any. I can remember we persuaded Keith Vallier who was the finance manager to try skating the unfortunate result of this was a broken wrist. I managed to become a fairly good skater and purchased my own roller derby skates (which I still have) and was later used on stage in a local pantomime."
Andy Gill (Coliseum Staff, St Austell, Cornwall)

"I also remember going to the Coliseum on National No Smoking day with Camborne Catering College on an educational visit in about 1987."
Andy Boddington (Plymouth, Devon)

"I was having a quiet pint while playing Asteroids one evening in the bar.
My game was going along nicely apart from this annoying man that piled his coins on the table (table type of machine) & repeatedly asked me how long I was going to be playing. My answer was obvious. Until I run out of lives. Eventually I lost concentration because of this idiot annoying me & when I stood up to let him play I was face to face with Alex 'Hurricane' Higgins. He was quite rude to me & sat himself down & proved he was much better on the snooker table than at Asteroids!!"
John Marsh (St Austell, Cornwall)

"Also the Radio One evening shows before the next days summer road show broadcast. I got hoisted on the stage with Tony Blackburn, DLT, etc."
Denis Bennett (St Austell, Cornwall)

The Cult @ Cornwall Coliseum
26th March 1987

Nirvana
Big Neon Glitter
Wild Flower
Love
Peace Dog

Electric Ocean
Revolution
Lil' Devil
Outlaw
Horse Nation
Love Removal Machine
Rain
Spiritwalker
The Phoenix
She Sells Sanctuary
Born to be Wild
Wild Thing
Louie Louie

Cornwall Coliseum

CARLYON BAY ST. AUSTELL SOUTH CORNWALL

★ NOVEMBER ★

SAT 21ST
NOV
7.30 p.m
£6
£5 (UB40 &
NUS)

W.O.M.A.D. PRESENT AN EVENING OF
AFRICAN MUSIC & REGGAE

+ SUPER DIAMOND DE DAKAR
+ RAIDERS 32 BURIAL CREW

REAL SOUNDS OF AFRICA

★ DECEMBER ★

FRI 4TH
DEC
8.00 p.m
£9
RAISED
STALLS
£8
ARENA

ALISON MOYET

FRI 11TH
DEC
8.00 p.m
£7.50
ARENA
&
BALCONIES

TERENCE TRENT D'ARBY

TUE 15TH
DEC
7.30 p.m
£8.50
£7.50
SEATED

Suzanne Vega

LOOKING AHEAD TO 1988

FRI 15TH
JAN
7.30 p.m
£10
ARENA
&
BALCONIES

MARILLION

MON 22ND
SAT 23RD
FEB
7.30 p.m
£8 £6 £4
CONCESSIONS
OAP/UB40
NUS

OPERA '80

BRITAIN'S LEADING TOURING OPERA COMPANY PRESENT

ABDUCTION FROM THE SERAGLIO
by MOZART   MON 22nd

CARMEN by BIZET   TUES 23rd

"I do remember seeing Toyah Wilcox, Hazel O'Connor, Siouxsie & the Banshees, being stood-up at Depeche Mode, Tears For Fears and so many more. One fond memory of Quasars was of my very buxom friend Nicola strutting her stuff on the dance floor, in a floral print frock. I remember saying to her if she keeps jiggling about next to me she'll bring on my hay fever!"

Jeff Barrett (Spain)

"When Sinead O'Connor was on top of the charts with 'Nothing Compares to You' I was working with the stage crew and my girlfriend was in the catering unit.
Katherine told me that after Sinead did her soundcheck she came into the portocabin, put on a pair of rubber gloves and helped out with the washing up as she wasn't bothered with going back to her hotel on her own."
Steve Savage (Perranporth, Cornwall)

Meat Loaf @ Cornwall Coliseum
13th February 1987

Execution Day
Blind Before I Stop
Masculine
Rock 'n' Roll Mercenaries
You Took the Words Right Out of My Mouth (Hot Summers Night)
Dead Ringer For Love
Midnight at the Lost and Found
Burning Down
All Revved Up With No Place to Go
Modern Girl
Paradise by the Dashboard Light
Bat Out of Hell
Rock 'n' Roll Medley

"Has to be Elkie Brookes, she was fabulous, but Cleo Lane and John Dankworth were awesome."
Pam Madge (Launceston, Cornwall)

1988

Another year and the introduction of another 'Aussie Soap' – TV saw the debut of 'Home And Away', 'The Phantom of the Opera' musical opened on Broadway, Al-Qaeda was formed by Osama Bin Laden, the 'Liberal Democrats' were formed in the UK and elected Paddy Ashdown as their leader, Benazir Bhutto was sworn in as the Prime Minister of Pakistan – the first female leader of an Islam dominated state, the Andrew Lloyd Webber musical 'Phantom of the Opera' opened on Broadway, the Iran-Iraq war came to an end, the movie 'The Last Emperor' by Bernardo Bertolucci won 9 Oscars, Enzo Ferrari – designer of the classic sports cars - died and Celine Dion won the Eurovision Song Contest singing in French for Switzerland.

The world saw the passing of Divine, the 'Disco Sensation' that was Sylvester, actor John Carradine, western author Louis L'Amour, Roy Orbison, and Andy Gibb, younger brother of the Bee Gees. In the world of music Adele, Skrillex, Hayley Williams from Paramore, Rihanna and Tulisa of N-Dubz were all born, as were Michael Cera, Emma Stone and Rupert Grint who would go on to play Ron Weasley in the 'Harry Potter' series of films.

The best selling single of the year in the UK and the Christmas number one were a 'double whammy' for Sir Cliff Richard with 'Mistletoe And Wine', a very rare occurrence by a 'British Legend'.

"We kicked off 3 UK tours from St Austell Coliseum, always staying in Fowey.
We also filmed our video for 'Road To Our Dream' from our 2nd album 'Rage' at Tintagel & the Coliseum. We had the very best of times at the venue, doing all our big pre production rehearsals there & always our first gig of the tour."

Carol Decker (T'Pau – Vocals)

"Back at the time of the tour we had with Magnum, we didn't really know the UK Club circuit that well so we don't have any particular memories from the Cornwall Coliseum. Nevertheless we're sad to hear the place has been demolished, this must have been quite a place in its time.
What we do remember with this our first tour in the UK is the good reception we got from both our fellow musicians Magnum and the audience. A rock band from Norway doing a tour in the UK was then almost as rare as Eddie the Eagle ski-jumping in Norway:-)
We got like 45 minutes and every night was like an exam, as you can't have a more experienced audience than the English.
As far as we remember it was all smiles, hopefully also at the Cornwall Coliseum :-)"

Torstein Flakne (Stage Dolls – Guitar/Vocals)

"I was in love, an unrequited love. I was in love or 'lust' with Belinda Carlisle, the raspy, wavery voiced sexy siren, ex of the GoGos and she was coming to the Cornwall Coliseum I could hardly control myself.
At the time I was on a photography GCSE course at college and one of our projects was to take photos at a concert. That evening I wore some jeans that had some extra room in them from when I weighed a little bit heavier and I dismantled my Canon SLR camera, removing the lens and separating it from the body and stuffing both down my trousers. I must have walked awkwardly, but I got in and waited my time for Belinda.
When she played she was awesome and I pushed my way to the front, reassembling my camera and snapping away for the most of her set. None of the bouncers said anything – they must have assumed that I had a press pass? – when she finished I left the venue with a film roll chock full of photos of the most beautiful woman at the time in pop/rock.
The following week at college we went into the dark room and I developed what turned out to be an excellent set of photos; not sure how I would have done if I hadn't dropped out of the college course, but it gave me a real taste for concert photography and I'm still taking lots of photos today."

Ian Carroll (Author)

"My 1st ever concert was here. And I have gone on to see loads

since. It was Belinda Carlisle and Breathe in 1988.
I used to love quasars as well!! It was the only place apart from
Secrets in Truro that was open until 2am."
Sophie Rowe (Falmouth, Cornwall)

"I know my mum saw many many live concerts down here and was
lucky that she took me to some as well.
However one concert which she didn't take me too was the
Belinda Carlisle one - have never quite forgiven her for that!!!"
Lou Thornley (South West)

Magnum @ Cornwall Coliseum
December 18th 1988

Vigilante
Start Talking Love
On A Storyteller's Night
Need A Lot Of Love
Wild Swan
How Far Jerusalem
One Step Away
Lonely Night
Days of No Trust
Don't Wake the Lion
Midnight (You Won't Be Sleeping)
Just Like an Arrow
Kingdom of Madness
The Spirit
Sacred Hour
When The World Comes Down

"Another good night was Magnum on the 'Wings of Heaven' tour. I roadied for them, got to watch them sound check in the afternoon, had a chat with Bob Catley & saw them for free in the evening.
And got paid!!"

John Marsh (St Austell, Cornwall)

"After seeing another excellent show from the classic prog rock gods 'Magnum' we went around to the back of the venue to try to get them to autograph our programmes.
We waited a little while and they came out and were all jolly friendly until I asked Bob Catley - the lead singer - if instead of signing his name he could draw glasses and a beard on one of his photos in the programme. Bob refused point blank which was a shame because I thought it would have been different rather than the repetitive autograph signing, he didn't agree, though we did get his signature instead...
After this I had a go at driving my friend Kev's car around the car park pissed. As I couldn't drive anyway it was all the more fun and I think Kev had food poisoning so he was being sick out the open back door as I swerved about, was fun though."

Ian Carroll (Author, Plymouth)

"I believe my first concert experience there was in 1988 when I was about 10 and it was A-ha, or at least that is my first memory of a concert. I remember before hand the excellent arcade and going to the Wimpy, I went with people in their teens so it seemed like a little world to explore with freedom from parents, everything great in one place.
From then onwards I went to various concerts such as Transvision Vamp and EMF, amongst others. I missed the legendary bands of the 80's, such as Motorhead, as I was too young being born in 1978.
I always seem to remember it was a decision whether to stay in the arcades and Wimpy or whether to bother watching the support acts.
I remember always getting a bit excited when I saw the jumping matrix men on the huge screen above the entrance, there was just something about it that said this is the best place to be in Cornwall.
I also remember the yellow t-shirts with the Cornwall Coliseum logo on that the staff wore, I have no idea why but I always wanted one.

I even remember going to see the wrestling there in about 1990 to 1992, the place was very versatile.
I also remember hanging around the back afterwards in the hope of signature from the bands. This rarely happened though.
Jon Read (Dorset, born in Falmouth)

The Mission @ Cornwall Coliseum
24th November 1988

Wasteland
Serpent's Kiss
Severina
Belief
Stay With Me
Kingdom Come
Deliverance
Tower of Strength
The Crystal Ocean
The Grip of Disease
Sacrilege
Dream On
Beyond the Pale
Like a Hurricane
1969
Dancing Barefoot
Hungry as the Hunter

Concert Travel Club

COACH PASS
MUST BE SHOWN WHEN BOARDING FOR BOTH JOURNEYS

1 1
COACH No.

RETURN COACH TO SEE MISSION ON TOUR **

ALCOHOL STRICTLY PROHIBITED ON ALL COACHES

AT   Cornwall Coliseum -ST AUSTELL
ON   Thursday 24th November 1988
DEPART Bretonside Bus Station -Plymouth
TIME   6.00 p.m.   YZ1A1109

PRICE   £ 3.50   RECEIPT

"I also have Rick Parfitt and Francis Rossi's autographs from when they dined at a Fowey restaurant.
Nancy (St Blazey, Cornwall)

"Went to see Status Quo with a group of friends.
We bought tour t-shirts and changed into them in the back of the car after the gig! Anyway main part of the story was that my good friends that I was with managed to hoist me up onto their shoulders. Quo were singing 'In The Army Now', the lighting was very stark, just white spotlights, but being up in the air I felt like they were just singing to me ...its was awesome."
Jan Pallett (St Austell, Cornwall)

"Also went to a Status Quo concert there. Again before the seats were put in. Memories of the plastic beer glasses pulsing with the loud music. Great to see my assistant bank manager was a head banger!"
Jenny Parnwell (Fowey, Cornwall)

Cornwall Coliseum

CARLYON BAY ST. AUSTELL CORNWALL TEL PAR (072681) 4004

SEPTEMBER

SATURDAY 17
7.30 PM
ALL ARENA & BALCONIES

SIOUXSIE AND THE BANSHEES

SUNDAY 25
10.30 AM TO 6 PM
ADMISSION FREE

BETTER DRIVING FUN DAY
IN THE CAR PARK
A DAY FOR ALL THE FAMILY
IN AID OF R.N.L.I.

TUESDAY 27
7.30 PM
ALL SEATS & ARENA

GOOD HEAVENS TOUR 1988
BELINDA CARLISLE
WITH SUPPORT ACT
BREATHE

FRIDAY 30
8 PM

JAMES LAST
AND HIS ORCHESTRA
SPECIAL GUEST
BERDIEN STENBERG
ONLY A FEW TICKETS LEFT

OCTOBER

SATURDAY 8
7.30 PM
£3 SEATED
£7.50 PROMENADE

THE RESTORMEL PROM
FEATURING ANNABEL HILTON
PROCEEDS TO CORNWALL AIR AMBULANCE

TUESDAY 18
7.30 PM
£7.50
ARENA & BALCONIES

T'PAU
PLUS SUPPORT
A CONCERT IN AID
OF GREENPEACE

THURSDAY 27
to
SATURDAY 29
ADMISSION FREE

RETIREMENT WEST '88 EXHIBITION
INCLUDES ASSOCIATED SEMINARS
COVERING ALL ASPECTS OF RETIREMENT
THURS & FRI 10am-5PM SAT. 10AM-6PM
SPONSORED BY WESTERN MORNING NEWS
AND AGE CONCERN

NOV

FRIDAY 4
TIME AND PRICE TO BE ADVISED

AFRICAN MUSIC FROM
TAXI PATA PATA
BRITAIN'S NO. 1 AFRICAN BAND
IN CONJUNCTION
WITH S.W. ARTS

NOVEMBER

SATURDAY 5

FIREWORKS DISPLAY
WATCH PRESS FOR DETAILS

TUESDAY 8
8 PM
£9.50 £8.50
£7.50

COUNTRY MUSIC SUPERSTAR
CHARLEY PRIDE

WEDNESDAY 9
30th ANNIVERSARY

CLIFF RICHARD
SOLD OUT

SATURDAY 12
8 PM

CLIFF RICHARD

SATURDAY 19
7.30 PM
£8.50 £7.50

HARPBEAT – THE HARP LAGER
MUSIC PROGRAMME
ELKIE BROOKS
IN ASSOCIATION WITH
PLYMOUTH SOUND RADIO

THURSDAY 24
7.30 PM
ALL ARENA & BALCONIES

THE MISSION

DATE TO BE ADVISED

OUTRAGEOUS NORTHERN COMEDIAN
ROY "CHUBBY" BROWN
ADULTS ONLY – STAY AWAY
IF EASILY OFFENDED

STOP PRESS .... STOP PRESS ....

MAY 1989

SATURDAY 13
8.45 PM
£10
£8.50

TOM JONES
TICKETS ON SALE FROM
30TH SEPTEMBER 1988

STOP PRESS .... STOP PRESS ....

"Then there was a 'mini market' that was there on Sundays for a few years in the late 80's."
Robert Adams (St Austell)

Marillion @ Cornwall Coliseum
12th February 1988

Slainte Mhath
Assassing
White Russian
Sugar Mice
Fugazi
Hotel Hobbies
Warm Wet Circles
That Time of the Night –
(The Short Straw)
Waterhole (Expresso Bongo)
Lords of the Backstage
Blind Curve
Childhoods End?
White Feather
Kayleigh
Lavender
Heart of Lothian
Incommunicado
Garden Party

"My friend Jude Husband and I went to the WOMAD Festival. I can't remember the year, but was in my teens.
We had very little money but was so glad mum trusted Jude to take me.
While mooching around the various stalls we found £50 and took it to the cafe, where the staff told us to keep it.
Awesome time was had!"
Lisa Nelson (St Austell, Cornwall)

"My local pub organised a trip to see Chubby Brown at the Coliseum.
On the way there a coach from Efford had broken down, so our coach picked them all up, all 50 of them!! (Wouldn't be allowed nowadays!).
Suffice to say our coach was well over crowded but the beer wasn't. We got there and I remember the man say "and now ladies and gentlemen Mr Roy Chubby Brown", to which I nodded off for the entire show only to be awoken with the cheers of MORE MORE MORE etc etc
Great day was had by almost all."

Rob Drury (Plymouth, Devon)

"Learning to drive in the car park and then Quasars, for us now legal aged drinkers and boogie beasts, then the name change and décor change to Gossips; how we all hated the name change, all we could talk about whilst waiting for the free mini bus picking us up, to take us there from the Holmbush Inn was, "...they've only painted the walls black and changed the name!"
By now we saw Gossips as an extra couple of hours drinking! However, we could dance and drink safely with all our mates (most of St Austell), although I was once "spiked", at the time you NEVER left your drink alone and always kept it covered with your hand. This one time I didn't and WHAM I passed out near the ladies toilets, a very strange experience. The most I was used too was a few Pro Plus (used before the discovery of energy drinks), a quick joint on the beach and a couple of distalgesics all taken with caffeine filled coca cola!! Not forgetting the fumbles on the beach before the bouncers caught you... if they test the ground and surrounding areas of the Cornwall Coliseum, most of St Austell's DNA will be found and we WILL be traced, now there is a thought, they'll know EXACTLY where we had been ;) the nights sat crying drunk outside my dad's workshop up near the wreck, the Zippy Burgers on the way home, there has and never will be a burger as good as a Zippy burger, FACT!"

Tami Cross-Halls
(St Austell, Cornwall - Aged 43 and 3/4)

"One of my first memories was seeing Aha in 1988. My mum took me when I was 10; I managed to get to the front as well.
My mum did panic when she thought I had fainted as she saw another girl wearing the same jacket as me with the same hair

Siouxsie and the Banshees
@ Cornwall Coliseum

The Last Beat Of My Heart
Turn to Stone
The Killing Jar
I Promise
Ornaments of Gold
Christine
This Wheel's on Fire
Something Blue
Scarecrow
Rawhead and Bloodybones
Carousel
Night Shift
Red Light
Peek-A-Boo
Rhapsody
Cities in Dust
Skin
Burn-Up
Trust in Me
Spellbound
Dear Prudence

Cliff Richard @ Cornwall Coliseum
12th November 1988

Born to Rock 'n' Roll
Move It
Daddy's Home
Devil Woman
All By Myself
We Don't Talk Anymore
Another Tear Falls
Some People
Marmaduke
Under the Gun
Ocean Deep
Living Doll
The Young Ones
Bachelor Boy
In The Country
Visions
All Shook Up
The Minute You're Gone
I Wish You'd Change Your Mind
Carrie
True Love Ways

My Pretty One
Miss You Nights
Thief in the Night
Blue Suede Shoes
Great Balls of Fire
Lucille
Long Tall Sally
Rip It Up
It'll Be Me
Mistletoe & Wine

"Sir Cliff Richard was another performer who thanked us and actually invited us back to the dressing room for photographs."
Sheila Gill (Usherette – St Austell, Cornwall)

"I should imagine everyone who was a 70's baby would have seen someone there (Cornwall Coliseum) in their teens.
Mine's a very random one as I had parents who liked Cliff Richard so my first one was him.
Once I had discovered my own music my friends mum took us to see Paul Young, OMG he was gorgeous in those days."
Debbie Westlake (Plymouth, Devon)

"Cliff Richard - I was never a fan, but many were, as they queued overnight to get tickets. He was in my previous opinion, just an average though successful singer, a bit cliché and safe. But was I wrong.
After the official sound check, he came back on stage before the doors opened and sang and played acoustic guitar for about half hour just to warm up. It was a real joy.
This was one of his pop tours, not gospel.
My opinion changed as the night wore on and Cliff put in a master performance, the highlight in my view was him bathed in a solitary over head spotlight, singing the Eric Carmen classic 'All By Myself'.
This concert won me over, he can really perform, a real superstar."
Jim O'Toole (St Austell, Cornwall)

"I saw the extremely talented comedienne Victoria wood there in the early 80's, she said it was the first time she had ever performed at a carpet warehouse!"

Alan Westaway (St Blazey, Cornwall)

"I knew my husband of 31 years from school but it was September 1983 when we met at Bentleys that we started going out together. A year later we married. Jemma our daughter came along in 1985 and Vicky in 1987.

On 14th May 1988 I was 38 weeks pregnant and went to watch Billy Ocean with Neil my husband and then sister in law. I popped to the loos near the end of the show and realised that my waters were going! Neil was not going to call an ambulance down there as everyone knew what it was like trying to get out after a gig.

We were in the top car park and I was dragged up the hill by Neil on one arm and Maria on the other, was bundled into the back of our car and then the mayhem started - everyone trying to get out, course Neil had his window down saying my wife's having a baby! Yea right!

Some of the stewards realised I was in the early stages of labour and stopped all the traffic to let us out.

The following day Thomas Raikes arrived a lovely healthy son.

Some very fond memories of the place including working with everyone when it was under receivership from 1996 -1998. Was such a fab place for us all in our youth, saw many big bands of the 80's loads of fond memories."

Mandy Raikes (St Austell, Cornwall)

1989

*T*he first major event of the year was the death of the Emperor of Japan – Hirohito – who reigned from 1926 to this year, Ronald Reagan retired from office after his second time as President and George Bush Snr replaced him, Sky Television was launched in Europe, Salman Rushdie released his controversial novel 'The Satanic Verses' and almost immediately went into hiding and Iran broke off relations with the UK as a result.

The Exxon Valdez spilt 240,000 barrels of oil into the water around Alaska as it ran aground, 'Rain Man' won the Best Picture Oscar at the Academy Awards, NATO celebrated it's 40th anniversary, Woodstock '89 festival takes place, the Hillsborough Disaster happened at the football stadium with the loss of 96 Liverpool supporters lives and 51 people died when the Marchioness pleasure boat crashed on the Thames.

Disney MGM Studios opened at Walt Disney World in Florida, British police arrested 250 people for celebrating the Summer Solstice at Stonehenge, the last episode of the 'classic era' of Doctor Who was broadcast on BBC1, Disney saw the resurrection of its cartoon feature films with 'The Little Mermaid, Steffi Graf and Boris Becker won the ladies and men's singles at Wimbledon, Nintendo released the Gameboy and in Thailand Mae Chamoy Thipyaso and her accomplices each received a prison sentence of 141,078 for a financial scam – the longest prison ever administered.

The world lost Salavador Dali, Daphne du Maurier, comic actress Lucille Ball, Ayatollah Khomeini, Laurence Olivier, Bette Davis, Lee Van Kleef – who was the 'bad' in the Clint Eastwood Spaghetti Western 'The Good, The Bad and The Ugly and Mel Blanc who provided the voices for Bugs Bunny,

Daffy Duck, Porky Pig, Sylvester the Cat, Tweety bird, Yosemite Sam, Foghorn Leghorn, Marvin the Martian and many more from the Looney Tunes stable of cartoon characters. Daniel Radcliffe from 'Harry Potter' was born, as were Avicii, Taylor Swift, Peaches Geldof and British swimming star Rebecca Addlington.

The best selling single of the year was 'Ride On Time' by Black Box and the big Christmas Number One was the remaking of 'Do They Know It's Christmas?' by Band Aid II.

"I remember the Billy Connolly show because he had no warm up act just went on the stage with a chair and talked. He was great although you didn't want to be at the front of the hall and go to the toilet."

Sheila Gill (Usherette – St Austell, Cornwall)

"I remember the Billy Connolly show mostly because I went with my father and my wife at the time, Mandy.
Having been brought up until the age of 15, in Glasgow, my father was a huge fan of Billy and he had many of his albums on vinyl – I always remember him not letting any of us listen to them when we were younger as they a 'bit rude'.
The show was brilliant, as would be expected, but there were two stand out moments for me – 1) It was one of the very few shows that I went to that was seated (the other being the Waterboys) and 2) it was the only time I went to a show at the Coliseum with my father, we nearly went to Tina Turner when she played, just before her career exploded again and made her a huge chart star, I wish we had."

Ian Carroll (Author, Plymouth)

"A more memorable evening was seeing Billy Connolly a special trip down from Barnstaple."

France's Deacon (Truro, Cornwall)

"I first went to Cornwall Coliseum in 1989 where I saw the Pasadenas.
I had seen them in the charts but they were fairly new to the pop world. My friend asked me if I wanted to go to, we were 16 and just left Newquay Tretherras.
I was surprised at how many screaming girls were there queuing when we arrived and when they came onto stage everyone the

crowd went mad.
I believe they still gig and are in their 50's now!"
Claire Schofield (Torpoint, Cornwall)

"Transvision Vamp in 1989 was great with Wendy James's raw punk attitude."
Richard Godfrey (St Austell, Cornwall)

"Most memorable moment for me was having a Rabbi come into the kitchen and bless a goat curry for a "Reggae, Roots and Rhythm" gig."
Kernow Lou (Barnstaple, Devon)

"Again, Billy Connolly' s great stand up show in the summer of 1989 had us all in bits."
Richard Godfrey (St Austell, Cornwall)

"I can remember doing the overnight security for the Custom Car show and was disturbed in the early hours of the morning by somebody banging at the window.
When I looked out standing there were about 5 or 6 uniformed police and two police cars they wanted to come in and look around. I thought that this would improve the security for the next hour while they were there, my only concern was that had anything else happened in the area all of the available police were there."
Andy Gill (Coliseum Staff, St Austell, Cornwall)

"This was a 'warm-up' for their Glastonbury appearance three days later. From what I remember it was all seated which usually annoys me, but didn't detract from the excellent performance on the night. Featuring many of the greatest songs including 'Bang On The Ear', 'A Girl Called Johnny' and the inevitable crowd pleasers 'Whole of the Moon' and 'Fisherman's Blues'.
I managed the see the band a few years ago at a festival and they are still as good as they were that summer evening at the end of the '80's."
Ian Carroll (Author, Plymouth)

"I remember seeing the Radio One 'Road Shows' in the 80's and walking from the top at Carclaze all the way to Crinnis Beach.
Before we got there we would go into the supermarket, the shelves were always very empty of alcohol and it was too easy to buy,

even if I was only 13 years old. Merrydown was the drink and so was Thunderbird.

As there was no security, there were lots of drunken youngsters running around.

Mike read would sing on air guitar and hit tennis balls into the crowd signed by him; Peter Powell would be always in the vicinity.

Bits & Pieces' was always an interesting all day event, if a DJ was on in the afternoon.

I saw Tasmin Archer and Nick Heyward. Would say about 1991, after the 'Road Shows' I avoided the Coliseum all together. Janice long did one 'Road Show' but mainly Steve Wright, Peter Powell and Mike Read when all was done 'Mr Angry' would say 'pick up all your rubbish' and then 'would say look at that person kicking that' etc. It did look a mess when the show was over. It was maybe why it was cancelled."

Robert Adams (St Austell)

"I remember the Saturday roller disco at the Coliseum. It was an awesome place to catch up with our friends and make "new" ones"

Claire Baker (Newton Abbot, Devon)

"My weirdest memory is being on the beach the morning after a night at Quasars watching some man flick giant jellyfish out of the water onto the beach with a pair of flippers!"

Lynnie Matthews (Torpoint, Cornwall)

"I used to go roller skating there in the late 80's. A friend & I bought 'speed' skates & being in our teens, it was a great way to eye up the boys!"

Angela Elliott (Penzance, Cornwall)

"Here's one that has to be anonymous I'm afraid to say, but the owner will know who it was!!!

We all used to be regular roller skaters Tues/Fri/Sat/Sun, in our teen years.

Anyway as life progressed, a few of us managed to pass our tests and get cars, basic though, Minis, Imps and Mk 1 Fiestas, Escorts if you had rich parents, anyway one night skating was heaving as per normal. So me and a mate skipped out for a smoke out front, past Ron Endean, he was great, we often did this for a bit of fresh air!

So, we get outside and spot our mates flash Mini, stripes, wide wheel arches, Weller wheels etc., all the late teens crap you could find in Motoring World as an extra! Anyway the mate I was outside with had exactly the same car so we came up with this ideal of 'would the door keys fit the same cars??'

So we wandered over, popped the key in the unattended mates car and there it was, 'click', the door opened, we laughed and said, "it would be so funny to go for a drive".

Anyway, fantasy turned to reality, IN ABOUT 15 SECONDS! And before we knew it, we were over the "wreck" end of the car park doing wheel-spins and handbrake turns and the longest skids we could, basically treating it like an ex-wife when she wants more cash!

Anyway, after 10 mins or so it was starting to smell a bit hot so we thought "oh shit we've killed it" so we quickly drove it back to where we had drove out of.

Now being kids, we couldn't, or hadn't even thought of the consequences of someone taking the parking space and guess who had come down parked in this space, yes Mr. G McNally with his Aston, or what ever his the big silver motor was. Anyway, now we were stuffed, how do you get the car back in the original parking space with McNally parked there!! Kids initiative!!

We managed to get the 4/5 cars parked to one side of McNally's by getting the cars all moved as we knew all of the owners who were in skating. I think the only person not to know about this to this day is the owner of the said Mini!!"

Anonymous (Cornwall)

"Remember seeing Billy Connolly about 1980, then Tom Jones, that was '89.

Women were throwing their knickers on the stage. He picked up a pair, gave them a sniff & suggested she should have washed them!"

Liz Walch (Plymouth, Devon)

"So many wonderful memories - my car (old Morris Minor) caught fire on my way down from Plymouth to see Tom Jones. Flames were coming out from under the dashboard and we had to stop to get help.
Still made it for the concert tho'!"

Julie Tucker (Perth, Australia)

Cornwall Coliseum

CARLYON BAY ST. AUSTELL CORNWALL TEL FAX (072621) 4804

16 APRIL SUNDAY
ONE NIGHT ONLY
SHAKIN' STEVENS
3.30pm £7.50 £7.50

26 APRIL WEDNESDAY
KING OF THE CROONERS
JOHNNY MATHIS
8pm
ONLY A FEW TICKETS LEFT £7.50 £8.50

29 SATURDAY
TOP COUNTRY MUSIC STAR
DANIEL O'DONNELL
7.30pm £7.50 £6.50

6 MAY SATURDAY
7 SUNDAY
CORNWALL GARDEN SHOW
MAJOR EXHIBIT:
"A FOCUS ON RHODODENDRONS"
SATURDAY: £4, AFTER 1pm - £3
SUNDAY: £2
UNDER 16yrs — £1 OR BOTH DAYS

13 MAY SATURDAY
TOM JONES
8pm
ONLY A VERY FEW TICKETS LEFT

20 MAY SATURDAY
8pm £7.50 £6.50
CLANNAD

26 FRIDAY
TO
29 MONDAY
IDEAL HOMES AND GARDENS
FRI & MON. 10am - 5pm
SAT & SUN. 10am - 6pm
ADMISSION FREE

26 MONDAY
TO
1 SATURDAY JUNE/JULY
THE BILLY GRAHAM MISSION '89
A 'LIVE' LINK UP FROM EARLS COURT LONDON

* TO BE CONFIRMED *
BANANARAMA
MAY 24 '89

"I have a few memories of concerts at this great venue two of which involve Irish 'folk' group Clannad. In 1989 the band played the Cornwall Coliseum on their then 'Past Present' greatest hits tour, the trouble was it was also FA Cup final day.
As you will know with the beach setting and the separate bar building it lent itself to a late morning on the beach and into the bar for the Cup Final on TV. Luckily the match (Liverpool v Everton) went to extra time, followed by a bite to eat and afterward our 'extra time' was the Clannad gig."

Graham Cooksley (Plymouth, Devon)

Cornwall Coliseum

WOMAD

FESTIVAL '89
25 • 26 • 27 AUGUST
£27.50
FESTIVAL WEEKEND PASS

JUNE/JULY	MONDAY 26 to SATURDAY 1	BILLY GRAHAM MISSION '89 — A "LIVE LINK" FROM EARL'S COURT LONDON. The doors open at 7.15pm
JULY	WEDNESDAY 5	THE FRANTIC AND FUNNY HARLEM GLOBE-TROTTERS
AUGUST	SATURDAY 5	THE LEGENDARY AND STYLISH GLENN MILLER ORCHESTRA

AUGUST	WEDNESDAY 9	BARBARA DICKSON
	SATURDAY 12	JIMMY JONES
	SUNDAY 13	I.O.U. THEATRE — "JUST ADD WATER"
	SUNDAY 13	ST. AUSTELL BAND
AUGUST	THURSDAY 17 to SUNDAY 20	HEALTHY LIVING EXHIBITION

AUGUST	WEDNESDAY 30	RADIO ONE ROADSHOW WITH STEVE WRIGHT

1990

*T*his year began with the US invasion of Panama with General Noriega surrendering to the American forces, the first McDonalds opened in Moscow, Nelson Mandela was released from Victor Verster Prison in South Africa after 27 years, the Brixton riots took place after a night of protests about the Poll Tax and Mikhail Gorbachev became the first Executive President of the Soviet Union.

The very first episode of 'Mr Bean' was broadcast on ITV, 'Driving Miss Daisy' won Best Picture Oscar at the Academy Awards, the Hubble space telescope was launched, the World Health Organisation finally removed homosexuality from its list of 'diseases'?!

Universal Studios Orlando opened its doors, the Berlin Wall was brought down, J.K. Rowling began writing 'Harry Potter and the Philosophers Stone' whilst she was traveling by train from Manchester to London Euston, 'Home Alone' was released at the cinema, the Gulf War began with Iraq's invasion of Kuwait, the first digital cameras were sold in the US, Margaret Thatcher resigned and was succeeded by John Major and Tim Berners-Lee invented the 'World Wide Web'.

The world saw the demise of Ava Gardner, Greta Garbo, Sammy Davis Jr, Jim Henson, Max Wall, Rex Harrison, Stiv Bators of the band 'The Lords of the New Church' and Melanie Appleby – one half of Mel & Kim. Kristen Stewart of 'Twilight' was born, as well as Emma Watson – Hermione from the 'Harry Potter' series of films, Jennifer Lawrence, Aaron Ramsey, Andy Biersack of 'Black Veil Brides' and Rita Ora.

The biggest selling single of the year was **'Unchained Melody' by the Righteous Brothers and Sir Cliff Richard was back at** *the top of the charts for the Christmas Number One with 'Saviours Day.*

"Haven't really got too much I can remember about that gig.
I believe I played there supporting Fish - Sandwiched between I think a Brighton date and an Aylesbury one.
Fish had hired those sleeper coaches so we travelled overnight to the gig and off again overnight to Aylesbury.
I think Fish organised a barbecue outside after the sound check - That's as much as I can recall.
It was a while ago I would guess 24 years - Am I thinking of the right gig?
It must have been a good gig as I tend to remember the bad one's better than the good ones.
Sorry I haven't got any other good stories."
John Otway (Vocals/Guitar)

Black Sabbath @ Cornwall Coliseum
September 10th 1990

Neon Knights
Iron Man
Children of the Grave
Anno Mundi
Die Young
Headless Cross
When Death Calls
War Pigs
The Shining
The Law Maker
Heart Like a Wheel
The Sign of the Southern Cross

Black Sabbath
Heaven and Hell
Paranoid

"It was the second time that I had seen Black Sabbath at the Cornwall Coliseum, this being nine years since the previous show and now with a different singer Tony Martin, giving the band a different slant. I much preferred Sabbath with Dio and Ozzy on his own, but this version was well worth watching. The crowd though was sparse and nowhere near as busy as the 'Mob Rules' tour and sadly due to poor ticket sales the last seven dates of this European tour were cancelled, which was a shame.
I had also come down to see the support band that I really liked, Circus of Power from New York and I used to play their album 'Circus of Power' – their debut one – to death, it being released in 1988, so I knew it well; it was a shame that they split up less than five years later."
Ian Carroll (Author)

"I remember waiting out the back after the Sabbath gig to meet them it was on the 'TYR', tour Tony made an appearance but only to pretend to walk on air."
Jeremy Wills (Delabole, Cornwall)

"The concert I have most memories of is the one I actually have photographs from. The fathers of Heavy Metal, Black Sabbath, played the Cornwall Coliseum on 10 September 1990, as part of their Tyr album tour. They were supported by Circus of Power. Again I was around the back of the Coliseum prior to the concert start. I watched the legendary drummer, Cozy Powell, arrive at the Coliseum. He was riding a massive motorbike, with no helmet.
It was here I met the man who created the classic Heavy Metal guitar sound we all know today, Mr Tony Iommi. I have a photograph of Tony and me. The image shows just how cool I thought I looked with my Poison tattoo. I'm dressed in a cut down Gun & Roses T-shirt and a pair of dodgy, tight, leather trousers. I also appear to have some sort of gold hoop stuck in my right ear!"
David J.B. Smith (Military Author – Plymouth)

"I went to the Cornwall Coliseum to see Jason Donovan in September 1990, because I had to take my sister as my mum couldn't go.
We stood by the pillar because we thought it was a 'focal point' and he might look out into the audience and see us and it would all be wonderful and everything.
It was a Jason Donovan concert so it was very good of course; I didn't want to go initially as I'm 'too cool' for that kind of thing, but it was good when I got there and then we got the bus home."

Holly Allison (Plymouth, Devon)

"In summer 1990 I went again, this time to see Jason Donovan who I had adored since my early teens when he starred alongside Kylie in Neighbours.
I had seen him at the Newquay BBC Radio roadshow and thought Wow!
At the Cornwall Coliseum he was amazing, he had a summer album out so we were all singing along between screams!
Brilliant night for us girlies."

Claire Schofield (Torpoint, Cornwall)

"Went to see Jason Donovan and Ray Wilkes let us back stage after (good family friend of my late uncle Preston).
There was a mini bus of disabled kids waiting out back to see him come out and get autographs; I think they had come from Liskeard.
Jason emerged from dressing rooms and was asked if he would go see the kids and sign autographs for them after being told they had come down just to meet him, and all the arrogant swine could say was "no way, I feel like a goldfish in a bowl mate". Utterly gutted children, and the end of my support for Mr Donovan!"

Lisa Nelson (St Austell, Cornwall)

"Janine Williams (was Turner) and I also went to a Jason Donovan concert there many years ago and saw him after we got off our coach (a Wallace Arnold one Peter Lucas my step dad also drove for them) he was cycling along the beach and came over to say 'hello!' I have good memories of that."

Tracy Stafford (Plymouth, Devon)

"I remember when my daughter was four we went to see Jason Donovan, she was such a fan we had a great night at the

Coliseum."
Tina Chadwick (Redruth, Cornwall)

Fish @ Cornwall Coliseum
3rd July 1990
Big Wedge
Assassing
State of Mind
Family Business
The Voyeur (I Like to Watch)
Punch and Judy
Slainte Mhath
Vigil
The Company
Kayleigh
Lavender
Heart of Lothian
Cliché
Fugazi
Internal Exile

"We had a lady stay (at the B & B) that had been to every single Tom Jones gig.... She was lovely"
Nancy (St Blazey, Cornwall)

"I still remember the magical moment of coming down the Coliseum road for the first time and seeing this big yellow building getting bigger and bigger, surrounded by the picturesque setting of the beach and the sea.
I thought to my self, wow this is special.
From that moment on I had a love affair with the Cornwall

Coliseum, from my very first time, which was a Vanilla Ice Concert to my final time, The Mega Dog Festival. The Coliseum will always be one off my favourite venues and settings. I've never been to a venue since, where the beach is virtually at the front door.

From arriving in the car park to entering the main doors and being greeted by the arena, I will never forget the magic that is The Cornwall Coliseum."

Wayne 'Spuddy' Small (Bideford, Devon)

"Fell in love for the first time with a lad I met in The Ocean Suite who was down on holiday from Birmingham. Had my first 'Wimpy' burger & went to the first of many Radio One Roadshows (my sister got on 'Bits 'n' Pieces!!!)

Baby Quazers, Gossips, Buddy's bar & Waterfront - all weekly social gatherings where, in a world when mobile phones didn't exist, you could guarantee to meet all your pals with no pre arrangements!

Many Sunday afternoons/evenings spent at the roller disco (wishing I had the best and coolest skates - never did get them!) and in the arcade.

Happy, happy days!!

My teenage years would have been very different without the Coliseum 'social hub' of every young persons social life! Oh, not forgetting the 'free' parking my sister could get by paying with a couple of 'Focus Points' from a packet of Embassy no 1! (I think the parking guy was saving for something special!) Good 'uld nostalgia!!!

Jude Williams (Dublin, Ireland)

"I took my parents to the Pogues' gig but thought that it would be better for them to sit in the balcony at the side, as there was a distinct whiff from the crowd, and wasn't sure if my mum and dad were open minded enough for that.

Shane was "a little worse for wear" so when he wasn't needed on the stage he was taken into the wings. We had a brilliant view of him while he staggered around until he nearly fell off the side several times and someone made him sit down until his next song. The gig was amazing and my parents loved it!"

Julie Lindsey-Cruddace (Padstow, Cornwall)

"In 1990, I was on holiday in Cornwall, from up country, with a friend and his family. We saw an advert for the Coliseum and

thought it sounded like the place to be on a Friday/Saturday night. So we set off in the car on the long trip from Perranporth. Unfortunately, on arrival we were turned away.

I can honestly say that it is the only time in my life that I have been barred entrance to a nightclub for being too old.

We were 17, and had turned up to an under 16s disco night! The giveaway to staff was the car we drove ourselves there in.

Looking on the bright side, we still made it into St Austell to join my friend's family at the cinema in time to see 'Back to the Future Part III'!"

Gareth Evans (Plymouth)

"Well I remember that they (Wet Wet Wet) or he (Marti Pellow) went to play golf before the show, & then wanted the massage.

He kept me waiting a couple of hours then with his charming big smile he undressed in front of me and I had a bit of a shock as he obviously believed in 'Going Commando', so I quickly threw him a large white towel & politely but primly said 'very nice please wrap this around yourself', when he lay down I gave it a sharp tug and he yelped as he must have tucked it in!!"

Pam Sekula (Gwinear, Cornwall)

"A Main memory about Thunder was the awesome opening music as they came on stage to AC/DC's 'Thunderstruck' also they played "Low Life In High Places' which had not been released yet. The date was 7th December 1990.

I remember the Irish band No Sweat supported them that night as me and my mates got to meet them afterwards they signed our program but had to sign over a photo of Thunder, as they were not in it themselves."

Jeremy Wills (Delabole, Cornwall)

Thunder @ Cornwall Coliseum
7th December 1990
Backstreet Symphony
Higher Ground
Low Life In High Places
An Englishman on Holiday

Distant Thunder
Love Walked In
Flawed to Perfection
Don't Wait For Me
Fired Up
She's So Fine
Until My Dying Day
Fly Me to the Moon
Dirty Love
Brown Sugar

"Me and my family went there a lot. One particular time we went to watch Suzanne Vega in 1990, I was only bout 11 or 12 and I was singing away and she looked over and smiled at me."
Melanie Finch (Liskeard, Cornwall)

"This is the only gig that I have stood at the back by the mixing desk, due to a person I was with was short, and they could sit on the barrier.... hell couldn't do that nowadays (H&S).
The sound was absolutely first class. The tracks 'Mandinka' and 'Jerusalem' sounded haunty, and her cover of Prince's track 'Nothing Compares 2 U' was just out of this world. The only downside of this gig was that pillar. Yes that pillar!"
John Lintern (Plymouth, Devon)

1991

The year started with killer Aileen Wuornos owning up to killing six men – her story was later be released as the film 'Monster' starring Charlize Theron in her Oscar winning role, Operation Desert Storm began in Iraq, Streetfighter II was released in gaming arcades, the Provisional IRA exploded two bombs in Paddington and Victoria train stations in the early morning and an amateur video was released of four Los Angeles police beating Rodney King – the police were eventually aquitted which led to the LA riots of 1992.

Comedy Central was released on cable TV, the very first Starbucks was opened in California, Winnie Mandela was sentenced to six years in prison for kidnapping, Boris Yeltsin was elected President of Russia and in a most unexpected event a member of the crowd was struck by lightning and died at the US Open.

The collapse of the country of Yugoslavia took place with Croatia and Slovenia declaring their independence, Steffi Graf and Michael Stich won Wimbledon, the Super Nintendo games system was released, Bill Clinton announced his intentions to run for President of the USA, in Russia the KGB officially ended operations, Magic Johnson of the LA Lakers announced that he had HIV, Conor Clapton, the four year old son of guitar legend Eric Clapton, fell to his death from an open window at their apartment on the 53rd floor in Manhattan and one of the saddest moments in music history happened when Freddie Mercury – the lead singer of Queen – announced that he had AIDS and died a few days later from pneumonia – the rock and pop world were in mourning.

People who passed away this year included Serge Gainsbourg, Michael Landon, Steve Clark of Def Leppard, Frank Capra, Dr Seuss and Gene Roddenberry the creator of Star Trek. Born this year were Pixie Lott, Ed Sheeran, Tyler, The Creator - of OFWKTA and Azealia Banks.

The best selling single of the years and the longest slot at number one in the charts was '(Everything I Do) I Do It For You' by Bryan Adams from the movie soundtrack to 'Robin Hood – Prince of Thieves'. Due to the passing of Freddie Mercury at the end of the year 'Bohemian Rhapsody' by Queen became the Christmas Number One.

Paul McCartney @ Cornwall Coliseum
June 7th 1991

Mean Woman Blues
Be-Bop-A–Lula
We Can Work It Out
San Francisco Bay Blues
Every Night
Here, There and Everywhere
That Would Be Something
Singing The Blues
O Sole Mio
Down To The River
And I Love Her
She's A Woman
I Lost My Little Girl
Ain't No Sunshine

Hi-Heel Sneakers
I've Just Seen A Face
The World Is Waiting For A Sunrise
Song In Space
I Like That Stuff
Maybe May Time
Hot Pursuit
Good Rocking Tonight
My Brave Face
Twenty Flight Rock
Band On The Run
Ebony and Ivory
I Saw Her Standing There
Coming Up
Get Back
The Long And Winding Road
Ain't That A Shame
Let It Be
Can't Buy Me Love
Sgt. Pepper's Lonely Hearts Club
Band
The End

"Went down in friends car (to Paul McCartney). Main car park was full, so was directed to park behind the Colly. Took nearly 2hrs to get out, as they emptied the main car park first before they would

let us out." **John Lintern (Plymouth, Devon)**

"My mother Daisy Dingle came from Charlestown in 1908, my Dad, Len Parker from Mt Charles 1905. They played tennis at the Coliseum in the 1920's, as did the King who abdicated; he used to stay at Carlyon Bay Hotel
I used to spend my summer holidays in St Austell and from the late 1940's until I became assistant in Restormel Architects Dept. from 1978 to 1998
I use to visit Coliseum throughout the 60's and 70's. Cliff Richard and Status Quo.
One special night in 1991 was when Paul McCartney did a special warm up
Night. As I remember all tickets were free as short notice I had a ticket through English China Clay Riding Club.
My children Matt and Vicky carried on where I left off, most weekends when it changed to a Disco, when we lived in Trethurgy. Sad to see the beach and building last summer."
Tony Parker (Thame, Oxfordshire)

"Paul McCartney, was excellent, but my father heard the tickets were going on sale and joined the overnight queue in the Coliseum car park and slept in a sleeping bag covered in a carpet to ensure he got tickets."
Lee Slaughter (St Austell)

"Paul McCartney loved taking the 'mick' out of the Cornish crowd. He said "Evening Me Dears" LOL"! He went through the whole show in a thoroughly professional effortless manner."
Gary Cocks (Falmouth, Cornwall)

"When Paul McCartney came down to play, the people waiting to come in were in the 100's and this was 4 hours before the doors opened.
I arrived there just as the tour bus was going round the back. I saw crowds of fans chasing after the tour bus and they were all stopped by security. I on the other hand held back and noticed all the press going round the side of the building to the bottom of the back steps which lead into the Coliseum I went round with them.
As Paul McCartney got off the bus all the photographers were all busy taking photos of Paul and Linda McCartney and the rest of his family and band. This left me free to look Paul in the eyes and

say something to him and the only thing I could say was 'Welcome to Cornwall Paul' he gave me the peace sign and said "Thanks".
When he went up to the steps to the back he tried the wrong door first.
What a day that was."
Geoffrey Harris (St Austell, Cornwall)

"I worked there for three years - with legends such as Chris Savage, Wendy Northcott and Phil Haig. I was also the designer for those crazy cartoons on the wall as I designed the menu for "Just-a-bite". My husband also worked there for about 5 years. Most miserable gig was Cliff Richard lol I cooked him a Jacket potato with mushrooms - blinding."
Kernow Lou (Barnstaple, Devon)

"Also in 1991 was Paul McCartney's gig which I had the privilege of seeing."
Richard Godfrey (St Austell, Cornwall)

"Way back in August 1991 (in a past life) I had my Wedding Reception evening 'do' in the Ocean Suite.
My ex-wife and I hosted a Dame Edna themed event, where we presented each guest on arrival with an alternative-name badge, as she used to do on her Dame Edna Experience TV show!"
Jeff Barrett (Spain)

"In 1991 saw Debbie Harry who did a great gig."
Richard Godfrey (St Austell, Cornwall)

"Loved going to Quasars on a Friday night after a week at school / college, it was the highlight of the week & always looked forward to it.
I'm actually struggling to remember the exact layout of Quasars, I remember going in with the stairs going up to the right, the ticket desk on the left where the nice older lady used to take your money, through the door into the main area & there was seating straight ahead, going round to the right there was a bar, then steps down to the dance floor with the DJ booth next to them, then another set of steps to the dance floor, followed by my favourite seating booth, then you went up some stairs, went round to the left & there was another set of steps up to the upper level, I think there was seating on either side as you entered the upper level, a

doorway leading to the main stairs, toilets & front quiet area, another bar next this doorway then at the back was the other quiet area/balcony, but I cannot remember if you could do a full circuit upstairs or it was a dead end, I remember it was altered quite a bit when it was Gossips with several seating areas gone & an extra set of steps to the dance floor.

Makes me feel old.

Made some good friends there but sadly lost touch with most over the years.

When I was 17, to my surprise, this girl named Amanda came on to me one Friday night, I'd been trying for 2 years to pull, & let's face it, who didn't go to Quasars without wanting to pull :D

So it was a nice surprise & ended up having my first kiss with her in the upstairs seating booths & spent the entire evening with her.

Also on that night, we stood at the front upstairs window watching the bouncers ejecting two lads for fighting over a girl, and there was also a massive thunderstorm going on.

On the way home back to Probus there was a car overturned at Trelowth just outside Sticker, as this was before the bypass was built we were stuck there for two hours, & I remember the police gave me & my friend a fluorescent vest each & asked us to flag down traffic so they didn't smash into the queue of cars around the bend.

So that was quite a memorable night, as for Amanda nothing came of it, saw her a couple of times in the Golden Penny arcade in St Austell & then never saw her again.

Back then I think you only had Secrets in Truro, & people used to come from Truro & the surrounding villages to Quasars as it was much better & had one of the best sound systems in Cornwall.

Went to Friday Quasars right up until I was 19, I know it's a bit old for baby Quasars but I had friends there & thought maybe there was a chance of seeing Amanda there, but she never went again after that night.

I did go when it was Gossips once, but it was not the same as Quasars & didn't really like it that much, plus my favourite seating booth was replaced with the DJ booth!

The opening of the Loft & then L2, Bunters, & Chicago Rock in Truro must have hit Gossips hard, it was a sad sight to see photos of it left derelict & falling apart, a real shame the complex could not have been saved. I also remember going to the Radio 1 roadshows, having a burger in the Wimpey & playing pool in the arcade."

Adam (Truro)

"I love the Alarm, always have, always will. I just think that Mike Peters vocals and his great song writing ability put the band head and shoulders above many others that were around in the 80's and 90's; I even enjoyed his short stint more recently when he was lead singer for Big Country. All that I remember about the show - and it might have been that I had partaken in a few too many alcoholic beverages – was that they played a virtual greatest hits set and that when the words said 'all cards are marked' in 'Where Were You Hiding When The Storm Broke' someone threw a whole packet of playing cards in the air; having been to see the Alarm a few times since, I now know that that happens every time at that point in the show."

Ian Carroll (Author, Plymouth)

Alice Cooper @ Cornwall Coliseum
October 3rd 1991

Under My Wheels
Trash
No More Mr Nice Guy
Billion Dollar Babies
Love's A Loaded Gun
Bed Of Nails
I'm Eighteen
I Love the Dead
Devils Food
Steven
Sick Things

Feed My Frankenstein
Cold Ethyl
Only Women Bleed
Wind-Up Toy
Ballad of Dwight Fry
Poison
Snakebite
Go To Hell
School's Out
Hey Stoopid
Elected

"After careful planning, we left work at a suitable time and Neil drove down to the Colly. To try and beat the traffic out of the car park we parked up at top of the hill in a smaller, but not well know parking area. Then it was only a short stroll down the hill into Colly`s complex. Quick bite to eat in Wimpey, then queued up to get in. Once in a quick dash to the merchandise stall to purchase the obligatory T-shirt which was put straight on over the t-shirt being worn. Then it was a case of a little push here, a little duck there until we got to the front. During, Bed of Nails, a large nail was removed and blood squirted over both of us, covering our newly purchased T-Shirt! As mentioned earlier, we had parked up the top of the hill for a quick getaway. Once the gig had finished, we got out quickly and ran to the car, and we where on our way back.... planned had worked as we were not stuck in the main car park. At this rate we where going to be home in time to get down to the nightclub in Plymouth...well so we thought. Whilst Neil was driving, he must have drifted off a bit, as the next thing was the car hitting the grass verge. At this point we thought that it would be better to pull over and get some refreshments. First opportunity was at Liskeard, so never did get back before closing time, along with fake blood stained t-shirts!"

John Lintern (Plymouth, Devon)

"Saw many gigs, most memorable Alice Cooper which took 3 days just to set up the stage."

Kernow Lou (Barnstaple, Devon)

"I performed there as a child at 'The Last Night of the Proms' event in early 90's with Pamela Darlington School of Dance. I was 12 so probably around 1991?"

Stacy Weeks (St Austell, Cornwall)

"I had always been an avid fan of Hazel O'Connor since she debuted as the lead character in the film 'Breaking Glass' so to see her in such a large venue, which was fairly close to me, was a dream come true.

Imagine all our surprise when we turned up to see that the venue was virtually empty, with probably only a few hundred people in attendance at the show; I think that they had even strategically placed tables and chairs in the arena to fill the gaps, but my memories of this are a little sketchy to tell the truth. The support band To Hell With Burgundy played to the near empty hall, when Hazel came on the crowd was no bigger.

Hazel played as if she were performing to a massive audience and so the show was amazing, with tracks like 'Eighth Day', 'Will You' and her version of the Stranglers classic 'Hanging Around'.

What made the evening especially excellent was that after the show I hung around and got Hazel to autograph a poster for me - which I had rescued from the Coliseum's walls - and she gave me a bloody great kiss too, which was nice."

Ian Carroll (Author –Plymouth)

Cliff Richard @ Cornwall Coliseum
20th March 1991

All Shook Up
Move It
Better Than I Know Myself
Saviour's Day
The Only Way Out
From A Distance
Where You Are
Discovering

Yesterday, Today, Forever
Lost in a Lonely World
When I Survey the Wonderous- Cross
Flesh and Blood
Make Me New
Shine Jesus Shine

1992

*T*he world was amused to see President George H.W. Bush being violently sick in the lap of the Japanese Prime Minister at a State Dinner' In Japan and then fainting, Paul Simon was the first artist to play in South Africa after the end of the cultural boycott, the Maastricht Treaty was signed and so founding the European Union and Mike Tyson was sentenced to six years in prison for the rape of Desiree Washington who was Miss Black Rhode Island.

'Barney' the large purple dinosaur and 'Friends' both premiered on television, Euro Disneyland opened in France near Paris – later changing its name to Disneyland Paris, six days of riots took place in LA over the Rodney King beatings – 53 deaths were recorded and $1 billion in damages were caused, the Cartoon Network was launched, the 'Freddie Mercury Tribute Concert' took place at Wembley Stadium and featured acts such as Metallica, Guns 'n' Roses, Def Leppard, Extreme, Spinal Tap, Robert Plant, Paul Young, Roger Daltrey,

David Bowie, George Michael, Elton John and even Liza Minelli.

Betty Boothroyd became the first female speaker of the House of Commons, the 'Tonight Show – Starring Johnny Carson' aired its last episode, the summer Olympics were held in Barcelona, in Australia Lindy Chamberlain-Creighton was awarded $1.3 million after a judge ruled that her baby had indeed been taken away by a dingo, Steffi Graf and Andre Agassi won Wimbledon and Denmark beat Germany 2-0 in Euro '92 – Denmark were the last minute replacement for Yugoslavia who were no longer a country.

Bill Clinton was elected the 42nd US President, a fire broke out in Windsor Castle and caused £50 million of damage, Disney released 'Aladdin' in cinemas, Czechoslovakia split into two separate countries the Czech Republic and Slovakia, the Prince and Princess of Wales announced their separation and in the USA CD's outsold cassettes for the first time.

The world of comedy was saddened by the passing of Benny Hill and also by the deaths of Isaac Asimov, Marlene Dietrich, Robert Morley and Peyo – Pierre Culliford – the creator of the Smurfs. Born this year were Jack Wilshere, Neymar, Taylor Lautner, Selena Gomez and good girl, gone bad Miley Cyrus.

This year was a double whammy for Whitney Houston, having both the Christmas Number One and the best selling single of the year with 'I Will Always Love You'.

"It was the Bank Holiday Monday in August.
We had just spent the weekend at Reading Festival and it would've been our first evening back if it hadn't been for another trip to the Coliseum to see EMF supported by the incredible PWEI (Pop Will Eat Itself), even though we had seen both of them at Reading only a few days before.
It seemed that a lot of people had travelled down from Reading as I remember going to the mens toilet and two members of the Farm were in there and in the arena I bumped into Clint Boon of Inspiral Carpets, who gave me the nod as we had bumped into each other a few times in the guest area over the Reading weekend.
Both bands were excellent as they had been at Reading, though I always thought that PWEI should've headlined as they seemed

much more popular and I liked them much more.
I do remember when I bumped into the Farm in the toilet that they were trying to show off, talking about groupies and such, looking over their shoulders to check that I was listening, but in the words of Shania Twain 'that don't impress me much'…"
Ian Carroll (Author)

"The Wimpy was a regular stop off if me and my mates were riding our various motorbikes and fancied a bite to eat and often spent a few quid in the arcade!"
Steve Wade (St Austell, Cornwall)

The Cure @ Cornwall Coliseum
May 1st 1992

Open
High
Pictures Of You
Lullaby
Doing The Unstuck
Just Like Heaven
Apart
A Night Like This
Wendy Time
The Walk
Let's Go To Bed
Friday I'm In Love
In Between Days
From The Edge of the Deep Green Sea
Fascination Street
Never Enough

Cut
End
Close To Me
Why Can't I Be You
In Your House
Charlotte Sometimes
Primary
A Strange Day
A Forest

*"Neil decided to take his girlfriend at the time, as she was a '**big**' Cure fan. Put tickets into wallet, then did other things during the day. Late afternoon, picked wallet up picked car keys up, picked girlfriend up. Drove down to Colly and joined the queue. When near front of queue, took out wallet, took out ticke...oh no, no tickets!!! Neil had only gone and picked up his brothers wallet, as his parents had only bought him and his brother identical wallets...so they couldn`t get in....imagine the drive home!!!"* **Neil Penrose (Dunfermline, Scotland – via John Lintern (Plymouth, Devon)**

"I missed The Cure! I really wanted to go, but couldn't get tickets as I was at college all day the day they went on sale.
Instead, I made sure I was working (at the St Austell cinema) on the night of the gig, so I didn't feel so bad about missing it :(
Those who went, including my then boyfriend, said it was an awesome gig, so that DIDN'T make me feel better!!"
Kerenza Jinks (Par, Cornwall)

*"Have to agree that the Cure gig was fantastic. I even remember seeing someone in the audience with black spiked up hair and smudged red lipstick, just like Robert Smith! :D
It really was a brilliant gig! They played all of my favourites at the time and it was a shame that the evening had to end. I no longer have my Cure t-shirt as I wore it out wearing it too often! Ha-ha! :D"*
Terry Jago (Penryn, Cornwall)

"I went to see The Cure; it was truly the best gig I had been too.
I only went because I was at a loose end for the evening and arrived at the Coliseum, it was amazing but I probably fitted in quite well with my hair all spiked up (using soap and crimpers) and my black outfit from top to bottom with lace up boats to the knees.
For the first time ever we sat in the stalls to the right of the stage, an amazing experience."

Tracy Banfield (St Austell, Cornwall)

"Experienced all my 'firsts' at the Coliseum.
Saw The Cure in '92 for the first time, ('Wish' tour) - still my favourite band and it was one of the best & most memorable gigs to date and I've been to many!"

Jude Williams (Dublin, Ireland)

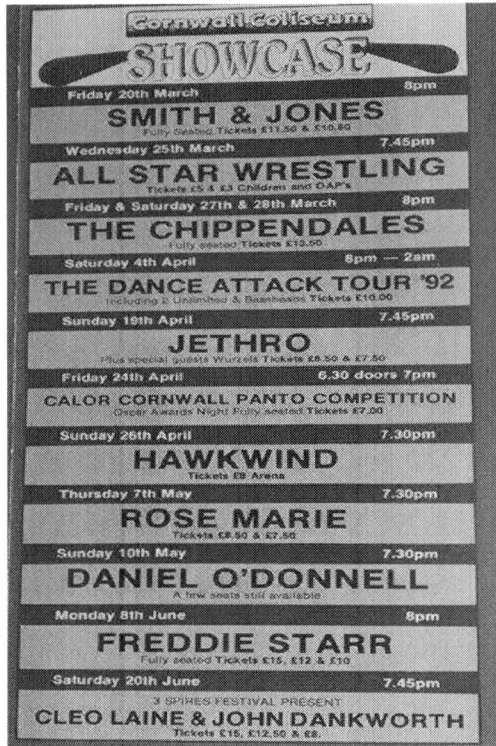

Cornwall Coliseum

SHOWCASE

Friday 20th March	8pm
SMITH & JONES	
Fully Seated. Tickets £11.50 & £10.80	
Wednesday 25th March	7.45pm
ALL STAR WRESTLING	
Tickets £5 & £3 Children and OAP's	
Friday & Saturday 27th & 28th March	8pm
THE CHIPPENDALES	
Fully seated Tickets £13.50	
Saturday 4th April	8pm — 2am
THE DANCE ATTACK TOUR '92	
Including 2 Unlimited & Beatheads Tickets £10.00	
Sunday 19th April	7.45pm
JETHRO	
Plus special guests Wurzels Tickets £8.50 & £7.50	
Friday 24th April	6.30 doors 7pm
CALOR CORNWALL PANTO COMPETITION	
Oscar Awards Night Fully seated Tickets £7.00	
Sunday 26th April	7.30pm
HAWKWIND	
Tickets £9 Arena	
Thursday 7th May	7.30pm
ROSE MARIE	
Tickets £8.50 & £7.50	
Sunday 10th May	7.30pm
DANIEL O'DONNELL	
A few seats still available	
Monday 8th June	8pm
FREDDIE STARR	
Fully seated Tickets £15, £12 & £10	
Saturday 20th June	7.45pm
3 SPIRES FESTIVAL PRESENT	
CLEO LAINE & JOHN DANKWORTH	
Tickets £15, £12.50 & £8.	

"Three years later Clannad were back at the Cornwall Coliseum and my wife (to be) patiently spent three hours afterwards whilst I got my CC gig poster 'liberated' from a wall pre show signed by the band, in fact I had missed one of the band members getting on board their bus so Moya the lead singer took the poster on board and got it signed for me.
Whilst recounting this tale to Moya at the Pavilions last year all the Clannad band members recalled "the venue in Cornwall on the beach."

Graham Cooksley (Plymouth, Devon)

QUASARS
CORNWALL'S LEADING NIGHTSPOT
A high tech, sophisticated, multi-level discotheque, playing the best sounds around with amazing light effects.
THURSDAY'S
FRIDAY'S
FRIDAY'S
SATURDAY'S
NATIONAL TICKET AGENT
Cornwall Coliseum
PAR (0726) 814004
Book in person
Book by Post (inc. booking fee)
Please note that special provision is made for disabled patrons — please advise when booking.
PORTH AVALLEN HOTEL
The ideal place to stay when you visit the Cornwall Coliseum. Our restaurant offers a full à la carte or daily table d'hote menu. Dine in comfort before the show.
WHERE TO FIND YOUR LOCAL TICKET AGENT
EURO BOWL
CARBIS BAY
ST IVES
TELEPHONE
(0736) 797136
FULLY AUTOMATIC • NINE PIN BOWLING
SNOOKER • POOL • ENTERTAINMENT
BUFFET/BOWL PARTIES CATERED FOR
THE COMPLETE SPORTS PUB
HEATHERBELL INN
CORNWALL
Coliseum
DOMAINE LEISURE
Shows to see
BOX OFFICE
(0726) 814004

1993

*T*he year began with the end of TSW, TVS, Thames Television and TV-AM, 'Monday Night RAW' began on television, two year old James Bolger was abducted and murdered, 'Unforgiven' won the Best Picture Oscar at the Academy Awards, female tennis star Monica Seles was stabbed in the back at a tournament in Hamburg and for the first time the general public were allowed entrance to Buckingham Palace. The privatisation of British Rail began and 'Doom' one of the first 'first-person shoot 'em up' computer games was released.

The world lost some legends this year in the deaths of Dizzy Gillespie, Rudolf Nureyev, Audrey Hepburn, Bobby Moore, James Hunt, Stewart Granger, Raymond Burr, Vincent Price, Federico Fellini, 'Carry On' legend Kenneth Connor, River Phoenix, Frank Zappa, Don Ameche and Bill Bixby who starred as Dr David Banner in the TV series 'The Incredible Hulk'. Born this year were Ariana Grande and Niall Horan & Zayn Malik of 'One Direction'.

The Christmas Number One this year went to everyones favourite Noel Edmonds creation (???) 'Mr Blobby' by Mr Blobby. The best selling single of the year was 'I'd Do Anything For Love (But I Won't Do That)' by the mighty Meat Loaf.

"DJ'd a wedding reception in the 'Ocean Suite' for (I think) the Rowlands fair people.
Half way through the night the groom had got off with one of the bridesmaids and the bride knocked him out cold.
Murry had to the kick the bride out of her own reception then 'all hell let loose'.
I was packed up and home by 10pm that night.
Memorable for the wrong reasons. Happy days."

Andrew Dean (The Electric Strawberry Disco)

"The Shamen were the latest 'enfant terrible' on the block. They had been in the top 40 with 'Ebeneezer Goode' and caused much controversy in the lyrics to the song, with it being loosely relating to 'Ecstasy'; the video even featured Jerry Sadowitz one of the most dangerous comedians around.
The support band were the incredibly popular Utah Saints (I even bought a long sleeved t-shirt on the night) who had the Coliseum dancing from start to finish and the Shamen carried this on throughout their set as well.
They filled their set with crowd pleasers such as 'Move Any Mountain', 'Boss Drum' (title track of the latest album), 'LSI (Love Sex Intelligence) and 'Phorever People'.
The dance crowd proved incredibly popular with the Coliseum and many dance events would be held there in the following years."
Ian Carroll (Author)

Peter Gabriel @ Cornwall Coliseum
August 30th 1993

Come Talk To Me
Quiet Scream
Steam
Across The River
Shakin' The Tree
Blood Of Eden
Solsbury Hill
Digging In The Dirt
Sledgehammer
Secret World
In Your Eyes
Biko

Status Quo @ Cornwall Coliseum
28th November 1993

Caroline
Hold You Back
One Man Band
Mystery Song/Railroad/Most Of the Time /
Wild Side Of Life / Rollin' Home / Again
and Again / Slow Train
Forty-Five Hundred Times
Junior's Wailing
Roll Over Lay Down
Rock 'til You Drop
Dirty Water
What You're Proposing
Whatever You Want
In The Army Now
Rockin' All Over the World
Don't Waste My Time
Roadhouse Blues/The Wanderer/
Marguerita Time/Living On An Island/ A
Mess Of Blues/ Break the Rules/
Something 'bout You Baby I Like / The

Price of Love/ Roadhouse Blues
Restless
Let Us Dance/No Particular Place To
Go/IHear You Knocking/Lucille/ Great
Balls Of Fire
Rock and Roll Music/
Bye Bye Johnny

"One of the most amazing experiences was waiting for the first WOMAD (World of Music, Art and Dance) festival to start. We were all ready behind the bar for people to start to arrive, when suddenly they did - in their hundreds. We quickly ran out of Tinners Ale, and Appletise - which seemed to be the "natural" drinks of choice.
All the thousands of people attending were so polite and treated us really nicely during the whole weekend. It was long hours and tired feet, but a particular highlight was an almost private viewing of Peter Gabriel warming up on the Sunday morning."
Alison Pearson (Nr Exeter, Devon)

"My mother-in-law went to see the Dreamboys down in the Cornwall Coliseum, the least said about that the better; I didn't have a ticket…."
Gary Martin (Plymouth, Devon)

1994

The year kicked off with two brutal attacks – figure skater Nancy Kerrigan on her right leg by an attacker, under orders from her main rival Tonya Harding's ex-husband and in Manassas, Virginia - Lorena Bobbitt took a knife to her husbands penis and chopped it off, she then left the family home and drove several miles before throwing his severed 'member' out the window into a field – after a massive search it was found and re-attached in a nine hour operation.

Green Day released their album 'Dookie' which went on to sell 20 million copies worldwide, the Winter Olympics were held in Lillehammer, Fred and Rose West were arrested for multiple murders at their home in Gloucester, the internet was connected in the Peoples Republic of China for the first time, 'Schindlers List' won the Best Picture Oscar at the Academy Awards and Steven Spielberg got Best Director for the same film.

Jeffrey Dahmer – serial killer and cannibal – was beaten to death by an inmate on 'death row' at the Columbia Correctional Institution and Nelson Mandela becomes the first Democratic President of South Africa. The Channel Tunnel opened after 7 years of work, serial killer John Wayne Gacy was executed by lethal injection in Illinois, O.J. Simpson – former NFL 'running back' and actor – is arrested for the murder of his wife and her friend Ronald Goldman after a 'low speed pursuit' through Los Angeles, 'The Lion King' was released at cinemas, Brazil won the World Cup 3-2 on penalties, Woodstock '94 took place celebrating the 25th Anniversary of the original festival and Ronald Reagan admitted to the world that he had been diagnosed with Alzheimers Disease.

Many famous passings took place this year with the deaths of Cesar Romero, Telly Savalas, US comedian Bill Hicks, John Candy, Richard Nixon, Jaqueline Kennedy Onassis, Ayrton Senna, Dick Sargent, Burt Lancaster, Fred 'Sonic' Smith of the MC5, Cab Calloway and the person who everyone of my generation will remember where they were when it was announced that he had died – lead guitarist and singer for Nirvana, Kurt Cobain. This year also saw the births of Justin Bieber, Harry Styles and actress Dakota Fanning.

The biggest selling single of the year was 'Love Is All Around' by Wet Wet Wet from the soundtrack to the hit movie of the year 'Four Weddings and a Funeral' and the Christmas Number One was 'Stay Another Day' by East 17.

"However when I got to about 13 I became much more interested in the rave scene over pop music and bands, so there was a few years I never saw any bands. Thankfully the Coliseum kept up with the times and when I was about 15 in 1994 I started to go more to the raves there, such as the Dance Planet promotions.

The place was perfect for it; the only negative was the lack of an all night license. I guess you could call my Cornwall Coliseum era 1988 to 1999.

Simply speaking, whether you went there for the concerts, raves, fast food, skating, beach, nightclubs, or road shows, you no doubt had an excellent time and got addicted. It is a huge shame it no longer exists, generations are missing out."

Jon Read (Dorset, born in Falmouth)

"I have many memories of all the amazing times at the Coliseum, one was when I took my mum to see Tom Jones as a birthday treat for her.

She had been a fan for years (not the underwear throwing variety thank goodness!) but I just went with her for the experience.

Tom Jones just blew me away that night ...I had never realised he had such an amazing, powerful voice and I've been a fan ever since thanks to my mum and the Coliseum."

Jan Pallett (St Austell, Cornwall)

1995

*T*he year began with a technological revolution with Internet Company 'Prodigy' and America Online offering Internet access on the World Wide Web to the general public, 'Star Trek Voyager' premiered on TV, Richie Edwards of the Manic Street Preachers went missing – never to be seen again, Nick Leeson caused the closure of Barings Bank after losing $1.4 billion on the Tokyo Stock Exchange and Yahoo! Search was found.

No British soldiers patrolled the streets in Belfast for the first time in 26 years, the Oklahoma City bombing took place killing 168 people and injuring another 680, the Space Shuttle Atlantis docked for the first time with the Russian MIR space station, the world got its first announcement about the DVD, O.J. Simpson was found 'not guilty' of double murder and the lowest ever temperature in the UK was recorded at -22.7C (-17F) in Altnaharra in the Scottish Highlands.

There were famous deaths in Donald Pleasance, Ginger Rogers, Harold Wilson, Lana Turner, Jerry Garcia of the Grateful Dead, Dean Martin and everyone's favourite witch Elizabeth Montgomery who played Samantha on TV's 'Bewitched' which ran for eight seasons from 1964 to '72. Born this year was Joey Bada$$, Calum Chambers and Jordon Ibe.

The Best selling single of the year was 'Unchained Melody' by Robson and Jerome and the Christmas Number One was the 'epic and dramatic' 'Earth Song' by Michael Jackson.

Jimmy Page & Robert Plant
@ Cornwall Coliseum

July 15th 1995

Whole Lotta Love
Bring It On Home
Ramble On
No Quarter
Gallows Pole
The Truth Explodes
Since I've Been Loving You
The Song Remains The Same
Friends
Calling to You
What Is And What Should Never Be
Break On Through (To The Other
Side)
Four Sticks
Kashmir
Blue Jean baby
In The Evening

"Later, in '95 I had the privilege of seeing Jimmy Page and Robert Plant there on the 'Unledded' tour, again another amazing gig with the outstanding memory being their version of 'Kashmir'.
I really hoped they would do 'Stairway' but I recall Robert Plant saying they couldn't do it justice so would never play it."
Steve Humphreys (Torpoint, Cornwall)

"The mother of my son, myself and a couple of friends went to the Cornwall Coliseum in July 1995 to see Jimmy Page and Robert

Plant.

We were pretty excited, I never thought I would see the closest thing to Led Zeppelin in existence and yet here we were.

I can remember saying that I really hoped they played 'Ramble On' and 'The Song Remains The Same'. They did! My son's mum - Kate and I had tickets numbered 00001 and 00002, we felt like VIP's!

As we wound down the cliff a racing green jaguar with the number plate A1 JPP passed us and I was pretty stoked to think I had just shared a bit of tarmac with my all-time guitar god.

The support act was The Sheep Shaggers who in reality were an acoustic Big Country. The crowd was impatient to get them over with and on to the main attraction. I remember they covered 'Don't Fear The Reaper' and it got their best applause all night. As a working musician I remember thinking how painful that must be especially if you've had chart success with your own material.

Led Zeppelin's 'Whole Lotta Love' riff started up and Jimmy goose walked on to the stage. Electric!

The gig was perhaps not greatly attended and the band carried on regardless, I can remember Robert Plant introducing 'Gallows Pole' as a local traditional song and then confessing that he'd used the same line the night before and that was up country!

I can also remember someone in the crowd insisting that Robert Plant owed him for an eighth of hash, which got annoying. Perhaps the best bit was watching the band begin 'Black Dog' under Robert Plant's direction yet collapsing in a heap. He insisted they would start it again and they did It was so good, you could hear the extra 5% going in and it was ace.

I'll never forget the gig, somewhere I have a bootleg of it a friend managed to get for me."

Andy Boddington (Plymouth, Devon)

"I went to see Page and Plant and standing in front of me was a chap from the night shift from where I used to work, I was too shy to say anything at the time but after really enjoying the gig, I took the next opportunity, coffee break at work, to go and chat to him about the gig.

Me and Kel have now been married for 16 years."

Julie Lindsey-Cruddace (Padstow, Cornwall)

"Big Country acoustic, preceding Page and Plant.... I was six feet from Jimmy Page! Simple Minds magic.... Nils Lofgren just before Christmas.... Robert Plant with the first computer controlled lighting

rig I remember.... loads more I can't recall properly. Happy Days!"
Chris Martin-Gathern (Dikanäs, Västerbottens Län, Sweden)

"Ocean World 1995. Penrice School and most of the St Austell primary schools put on a huge joint production at the Coliseum. I was in Year 7 at the time and was part of the cast. I think my mum still has the video that was produced to this day!"
Sheena Uslu (St Austell, Cornwall)

"My last memory was Danceplanet 1995, Detonator 8, I did fall ill at this one, but the St John ambulance took great care of me and one of the ambulance men came back out with me when I felt better only to borrow my glow sticks and rave away lol!!"
Lou Thornley (South West)

Van Morrison @ Cornwall Coliseum
2nd September 1995

Tell Me How Do You Feel
I Will Be There
Melancholia
Perfect Fit
Sack O' Woe
Who Can I Turn To (When Nobody Needs Me)
Satisfied
Stormy Monday/Ordinary People
Help Me
Vanlose Stairway/Trans-Euro – Train

Moondance / Fever
That's Life
Tupelo Honey / Why Must I -Always
Explain
In The Garden / Daring Night / Real
Real Gone
You Don't Know Me
Have I Told You Lately

"What was wrong with going to see East 17? They had done some great 'pop tunes', they filled the venue out and because most of the crowd was under 16 it was gig that I could see right across the crowd from the back, which was a first.

The band all abseiled down from the ceiling onto the stage in camouflage gear and proceeded to play all the hits to the screaming girls, the parents and me and my friend Mike.

Mike bought the tickets for me for my birthday, but I'm sure that he really got them because he was a 'secret' Peter André fan - he was one of the support acts and I'm sure I caught Mike screaming whilst the 'Petester' sang 'Mysterious Girl'; if their eyes had met across the arena floor I'm sure that I would have found myself walking home…" **Ian**
Carroll (Author, Plymouth)

"The other time I went was to see East 17 and their support, one of them, was Peter Andre.

It was a lovely day, I'm sure it was a sunny day as well and it was definitely in the arena and it was good until Peter Andre came on.

I think I went with my mate Ian (the Author). I actually bought the ticket for him for his birthday because Ian really wanted to go and see Peter Andre, he was a big fan, he was dressed as Peter Andre just in his y-fronts and waving them around.

There were a lot of teenage girls there and we stood at the back with the parents - it was a bonus that East 17 were there as well and they were pretty good as it was the 80's, I mean 90's - wasn't it? Mmm Mmm? It was definitely about '95, I remember it clearly."

Mike Horton (Plymouth, Devon)

1996

*T*he year started on a high with France declaring that they would be ending their nuclear weapon testing, chess computer 'Deep Blue' defeated Garry Kasparov for the first time – only for him to beat it a week later, the oil tanker Sea Empress ran aground in Wales shedding 73,000 tonnes of crude oil, Pokemon Red & Green were released in Japan starting the Pokemon craze and Alanis Morisette won album of the year at the Grammy Awards.

The 'Dunblane School Massacre' took place in Scotland with the murder of 16 schoolchildren and one teacher and then the death of the 'shooter' Thomas Hamilton who took his own life, the Mel Gibson film 'Braveheart' won the Best Picture Oscar at the Academy Awards, the 'Unabomber' Theodore Kaczynski was arrested in Montana and FIFA announced that the 2002 World Cup would be the first joint one, to be held by South Korea and Japan.

A huge IRA bomb exploded in Manchester injuring over 200 people, Archbishop Desmond Tutu retired, Nintendo released the N64 games system, Martina Hingis won Wimbledon at the age of 15, the Princes Trust concert was held in Hyde Park and headlined by the Who, the last of the 'Magdalene Asylums' in Ireland was closed, Germany won Euro '96 in England – beating Czech Republic 2-1, Dolly the sheep was born – the first cloned animal and the Ramones played their last ever show.

The world saw the demise of many famous people and stars this year including Francois Mitterrand, Gene Kelly, P.L. Travers who wrote 'Mary Poppins', Carl Sagan and Tiny Tim who was famous for his crazy version of 'Tip Toe Through The Tulips'. Tyger Drew-Honey of BBC television's 'Outnumbered' was born, as well as singer Lorde.

The best selling record of the year was 'Killing Me Softly' by the Fugees and the Christmas Number went to the Spice Girls with '2 Become 1'.

"Went to 'Surfers Against Sewage Ball' with Reef and Underworld, it must have been '96. We were all dressed as pirates. It was last time it was held there and was then passed to Newquay.
Gossips was a usual haunt after a lot of alcohol.
Then getting a taxi even though we could hardly stand and drinking Merrydown we had smuggled in and then going around helping ourselves to pints 'we found'. There was a real party atmosphere after a few pints and it was packed drunken youngsters.
Even the security guy would swing his thing on the dance floor.
Bit of Van Morrison and the 'Grease Megamix' with a few new tracks did the job.
No mobiles in those days just good honest fun."

Robert Adams (St Austell)

1997

*P*resident Clinton was sworn in as President of the USA for the second time, divorce became legal in the Republic of Ireland, 'Midsomer Murders' began broadcasting on ITV, 'The English Patient' won the Best Picture Oscar at the Academy Awards and the cult 'Heaven's Gate' took part in a mass suicide in their compound with 39 people dying.

The 'Teletubbies' was shown for the first time on BBC2, the first 'space burial' ceremony took place when 24 peoples ashes were sent into orbit by a 'Pegasus' rocket, Gianni Versace was murdered by serial killer Andrew Cunanan and Tony Blair won the general election with a landslide victory and became Prime Minister for the first time – with the Labour Party back in power for the first time in 18 years.

Katrina and the Waves won Eurovision with 'Love Shine A Light' – the last UK win, 'Harry Potter and the Philosophers Stone' was released, Disney released their 35th feature length cartoon 'Hercules', Hong Kong was returned to China, Microsoft bought a $150 million share of Apple Computers and Steve Jobs returned to the company, 'South Park' started broadcasting on Comedy Channel and the summer news was filled with the death of Princess Diana.

The world lost Jacques Cousteau, Robert Mitchum, James Stewart, Mother Teresa, football legend Billy Bremner and Shirley Crabtree who was better known as the wrestler 'Big Daddy'. Chloë Grace Moretz was born and so were Rebecca Black ('Friday') and Daniel Crowley.

The best selling single of the year was 'Candle In The Wind '97' by Elton John – which was his original hit reworded for his friend Princess Diana's funeral and the Christmas Number

One was the second year in a row by the Spice Girls with 'Too Much'.

"For some reason this year seemed to be one of the least popular in the history of the Cornwall Coliseum. No one sent me any memories of events at the venue this year, no bands wanted to share their memories. It was the beginning of the end for the venue that we all had loved for years and years, through our youth and into adulthood.
The venue was still being used for dance music gigs and even Christian rock gigs, but the Pavilions in Plymouth was now the place that bands wanted to play and St Austell seemed to be just that little bit too far to travel; sad times were ahead."
Ian Carroll (Author, Plymouth)

Delirious? @ Cornwall Coliseum
6th November 1997

Sanctify
Come Like You Promise
Promise
Summer of Love
Hands of Kindness
King or Cripple
I'm Not Ashamed
King of Fools
Obsession
History Maker
All the Way

Deep

1998

This was the International Year of the Ocean, the Winter Olympics were held in Nagano, Japan, a massacre in Likoshane started the Kosovo War, Billy Crystal hosted the Academy Awards and the Best Picture Oscar was won by 'Titanic' which won a total of eleven Oscars, Disney's Animal Kingdom opened in Orlando, Florida and Bear Grylls – at only 23 years old - became the youngest British climber to climb Everest.

Windows 98 was released, J.K. Rowling released her book 'Harry Potter and the Chamber of Secrets', France won the World Cup 3-0 beating Brazil, the Omagh Bombing took place in Northern Ireland, Google Inc was established and the first movie from DreamWorks was released which was 'Antz'

Passing this year were Lloyd Bridges, Pol Pot, Frank Sinatra, Maureen O'Sullivan and everyone's favourite chimp Roddy McDowall who played Caesar in the 'Planet of the Apes' films and starred as Galen in the subsequent TV show.

The Best Selling single of the year was the song that made the most use of 'autotune' so far - 'Believe' by Cher and it was a 'hat trick' for the Spice Girls with their third year in the Number One spot at Christmas with 'Goodbye'.

"Once again this year the concerts dwindled and with it so did the memories, though from the 'pieces' that I received from people this year it was certainly a feeling of 'love is in the air' as people were falling in love still at Gossips nightclub which was still a popular weekend venue for people local to the area."
Ian Carroll (Author, Plymouth)

"I met my husband there 17 years ago, in the nightclub, at the bar...
Together still now even, we celebrated our seven wedding

anniversary last weekend...."
Ali Johns-Clemo (St Austell, Cornwall)

"I also met my husband 1st May 1998 and had our first kiss on the dance floor in Gossips nightclub, was a bet by all accounts!!"
Stacy Weeks (St Austell, Cornwall)

"I went to a Blues Brothers tribute night there. They had a raffle to win "the Bluesmobile". It was actually a knackered Ford Cortina painted black and white with a couple of dustbins on the roof. I didn't buy a ticket."
Roger Lambshead (Cornwall)

"I also got together with my Wife, Lisa (was Lisa Best) at Gossips Nightclub at Carlyon Bay in June 1998 & here we are 17 years later with 2 x children aged 12 & 10 (Robert & Michael Slaughter) after having been married for 13 years."
Lee Slaughter (Par, Cornwall)

"Went with my sister and mum to see Shakin' Stevens probably in the late seventies and before that Franki Vaughn on stage and also it became the home of St Blazey Operatic Society's annual Pantomime for a while in the Coliseum about 1998."
Patricia Darch (St Austell, Cornwall)

1999

This was the year that the 'Euro' was established – saying a sad farewell to - amongst many currencies - Francs, Pesetas and Deutschmarks, 'Family Guy' made its debut on Fox in the USA, the Mandalay Bay Hotel opened in Las Vegas, the 71st Academy Awards was held in Los Angeles and the Best Picture Oscar was won by 'Shakespeare In Love', Bill Gates was announced as being the wealthiest man in the world, TV presenter Jill Dando was shot dead on her doorstep in Fulham, London and David Copeland 'the London Nail Bomber' caused havoc by setting off devices in areas frequented by the Asian, black and gay communities.

'Spongebob Squarepants' was on TV for the first time on Nickelodeon', at cinemas 'Star Wars Episode 1: The Phantom Menace' was released, Manchester United won the UEFA Champions League beating Bayern Munich 2-1, the first version of 'Microsoft Messenger' was released, Woodstock '99 was held in the USA, the total solar eclipse took place in Europe and Asia, Grand Theft Auto 2 was released on the Playstation, in Russia President Boris Yeltsin resigned with Prime Minister Vladimir Putin filling the gap and George Harrison was attacked by an intruder and he suffered 40 stab wounds and head injuries.

The world lost Stanley Kubrick, baseball legend Joe DiMaggio, DeForest Kelly who played Bones in the original 'Star Trek' TV series, violinist Yehudi Menuhin and Desmond Llewwlyn who played the character of 'Q' in seventeen of the James Bond films. Daniel Roche who played Ben in BBC1's 'Outnumbered' was born, as were Chandler Riggs who plays Carl Grimes in 'The Walking Dead' and Yui Mizuno and Moa Kikuchi both of the Japanese band 'Babymetal'.

The best selling single of the year this year was '…Baby One More Time' Britney Spears which launched her career and the

Christmas Number One was the double cover single, covering ABBA and Terry Jacks with 'I Have A Dream/Seasons In The Sun' by Westlife.

"The venue was now beginning to wind up. Gary Barlow played prior to his much more successful return to stadiums with Take That and Hawkind, Blondie and Suede all played the hall trying to return to the venues halcyon days. But the writing was on the wall. The Pavilions in Plymouth had now destroyed the Coliseum and the gigs became less frequent with most acts not travelling into Cornwall to play. The end of the venue was now on the cards...."
Ian Carroll (Author, Plymouth)

"Gary Barlow in late 1999 who was one of the last big acts to perform at the Cornwall Coliseum and the main hall was over half empty."
Lee Slaughter (St Austell)

"I went to see Gary Barlow with my sister and sister-in-law. We had a great night."
Jeanette Hayes (Camborne, Cornwall)

"The last band I saw was Suede, who were bloody good, which must of been around 1999?!!"
Steve Wade (St Austell, Cornwall)

"My last was Dr. Feelgood in the small venue just before it closed."
Mike Bennett (Cornwall)

"Hawkwind – my mate got me to go and see them rather than Blondie which was on the next night. Hawkind didn't play 'Silver Machine' – total crap.I have never forgiven my mate to get me to go to that concert, Blondie in that era was top notch and I missed that concert!!!"
K.N. Nankivell (Bodmin, Cornwall)

All looking quiet and nearing
The End

2000

A new year and the start of a new 'Millennium' and the first new 'Century Leap Year' since 1600.

The year began with Israel and Syria holding peace talks, the final 'Peanuts' cartoon strip was published following the death of Charles M. Schulz, Playstation 2 was released, Vladimir Putin was elected President of Russia, the Billionth living person was born in India and the Tate Modern Gallery opened for the first time in London.

The first short film '405 the Movie' was released on the internet making it the first 'viral film', France won the Euros – beating Italy 2-1 after extra time, the world was introduced to the Nintendo 'Game Cube', the summer Olympics were held in Sydney, a gang were caught in the Millenium Dome trying to steal the 'Millenium Diamond and the Millenium closed its doors on New Years Eve – the next time it would open it would be the O2 Arena.

Actress Hedy Lamarr died this year, as did Walter Matthau, Ian Dury, Barbara Cartland, Doris Hare who played Mum in 'On The Buses', David Tomlinson, Sir Alec Guiness, Reggie Kray and Jim Varney who starred as Ernest P. Worrell in the series of comedy films.

It was a double for the Best Selling Single of the Year and the Christmas Number One with 'Can We Fix It?' by Bob The Builder.

"It was a sad night, although I didn't realise it at the time, March 10th 2000 would be the last time that I saw a gig at the Cornwall

Coliseum, this time in the small venue above the Wimpy – The Waterfront.

It was a small venue and it was packed to the rafters with rock and metalheads. Terrorvision were still popular, though they had lost their record contract and were now bringing material out themselves.

Playing a set that included favourites like 'Perseverance', 'Oblivion', 'Celebrity Hit List', 'Pretend Best Friend', 'Alice, What's The Matter' and more, Tony and the boys were incredibly popular and the night was a great success.

As I left the venue, heading back to the car, little did I know that the next time that I would visit the venue was just to see what kind of shape it was in – and it wasn't good - on the night when the Kaiser Chiefs played at the Eden Sessions for the first time and we had time to kill.

A great gig, but a sad end to my Coliseum gig attending career, nineteen years after the first time I attended and forty two gigs later."

Ian Carroll (Author)

2005

The year began with North Korea announcing that it now had nuclear weapons, YouTube was founded, Pope John Paul II passed away, MG Rover went out of business and Pope Benedict XVI and Kuwaiti women were re-granted the right to vote.

Live 8 took place in ten simultaneous concerts all around the world – opened in the UK by Paul McCartney with U2, the UK won the rights to host the 2012 Olympic Games, terror attacks took place in London on July 7th on the bus and the underground, the Provisional IRA announced that the campaign of terror was over – which had been continuing since 1969, Hong Kong Disneyland opened, the trial of Saddam Hussein began and the first fully computer animated feature film by Disney "Chicken Little' was released.

The was lost Virginia Mayo, Johnny Carson, James Callaghan (former UK PM), Prince Rainier III of Monaco, Eddie Albert, Edward Heath, Pat Morita from 'the Karate Kid' and comedy LEGEND Richard Pryor.

The Best Selling single of the year was for the 'Children in Need' charity release 'Is This The Way To Amarillo?' by Tony Christie feat. Peter Kay and the Christmas Number One was the 'X-Factor' winner Shayne Ward with 'That's My Goal'.

"So I have a story, it happens on the bank holiday weekend in 2005.
Well At the end of 2004 I moved to Bath.
Not a million miles away from the home of my parents in St Austell.
So fast forward to May 2015.
My friend Chris was gonna get married at the hotel in Carlyon bay.
I didn't have a date, but it was a really nice wedding; as I am writing this it's their 10th wedding anniversary tomorrow.
Well, it came to about 1130 and as I was driving, decided to set off

back home. So I drive along the main road it was really peaceful and quiet and before I got to the shops I see a woman, wearing an ice hockey Jersey thumbing for a lift.

Well being that it's St Austell I thought she looks about my age so I'll stop and see if she wants a lift towards town.

Well I stopped and wound down the window.

And I knew the woman, she was a nice girl, but she had some issues in her life and had done some silly things in her past.

Well I said " hey Nikki "

She replied with "hell I haven't seen you in years how you been?"

I then asked " what you doing hitching up in Carlyon Bay?"

Her response " I've not lived in St Austell for bout 9 years, I came down to visit my parents, I thought I'd go down to Gossips for a mosh. but these security guards turned me away,"

She thought there was a rave on and she was being turned away for not having a ticket.

"Erm Gossips closed 2 years back and the Coliseum is in disrepair," I informed her. She still looked confused so I drove her in to town to her mate's house."

Richard Winterburn (Bristol)

Epilogue- 2015: "The End"

"It's a very sad day when something that you've grown up with and spent such great times at is no more and that is now the case for the Cornwall Coliseum.
The place where I spent so much of my youth at is now a sandy empty space, next to the beach at Crinnis.
The beach bar at the far end of the beach has mementoes, signs plastered around the walls which hark back to those times gone by, keeping the memories alive of the greatest venue that the south west ever had – the sign is on the cover of this book.
Gone, but not forgotten, RIP Cornwall Coliseum…"
Ian Carroll (Author)

"I was sad to hear it was no longer used & finally demolished. Its part of T'pau's history."
Carol Decker (T'Pau – Vocals)

"Sadly the Cornwall Coliseum has met its demise, but during it's time it provided the perfect venue for concert goers to enjoy a night out seeing their favourite bands."

Mark Jewitt (Plymouth, Devon)

"Cornwall Coliseum was a fantastic venue with the beach and many fond memories. It should never have been sold off and demolished."

Harry Harris (Torpoint, Cornwall)

"Then we moved away, married and had babies, visited the Cornwall Coliseum occasionally for a boogie, then gradually we began to look old and uncomfortable. We then stopped going, and the next and the last generation had memories made.
The last time I visited the Cornwall Coliseum was this year a week before she was pulled down, to say goodbye and thank her for being there for my safe childhood. One of the last generations to have a true outdoor, safe and "he's a dirty old man, so stay away" knowledge childhood.
No mobile phones, you came in when you were hungry or the streetlights went on, no computer games, only bikes and a lot of imagination.
So, times have changed, it's now 'her' time, no matter how sad we all are.
RIP Cornish Riviera, Carlyon Bay, Cornish Coliseum and many other names."

Tami Cross-Halls
(St Austell, Cornwall - Aged 43 and 3/4)

"With the Venue, The Coliseum and the complex together, it made it a world-class site. Some stars I've met all said that the venue had the best acoustic sound they'd ever played in. It's such a same that it was left to rot for so many years and I cannot believe it was demolished and 'run of the mill' apartments are going to ruin the natural beautiful tone of the place."

Gary Cocks (Falmouth, Cornwall)

"I had seen a lot of great bands there.
The thing I took note of was that all bands wanted to play there. It was a crucial part of everyone's UK and world tours. It's sad to think there is nowhere now with the draw this building used to have."

Adrian Dennis (Cornwall)

"I was there the first day they started the demolition, a sad day but inevitable I suppose. Good times."
Mike Bennett (Cornwall)

"RIP Cornwall Coliseum – gone maybe but the happy hours spent there will not be forgotten by many."   **Derek Hore (Paignton, Devon)**

"Sad to see the old place go, but it had declined over the years due to lack of investment.
My wish would be for a new Coliseum to be born on Par Moor or somewhere. Wouldn't it be great... the fact that The Club was packed when we had the Reunion, proves that there are enough older people who still want to dance and jive to make something like that work."
Stephen Nott (St Austell, Cornwall)

"Just an amazing place, badly missed as nowhere has taken its place down here."
Sharon Elston (Exeter, Devon)

"I witnessed many of my formative bands in concert at the Cornwall Coliseum. This venue by the sea was instrumental in shaping a love for Heavy Metal music, which I still consider a guilty pleasure today.
However sad it was to see the Coliseum being demolished, I console myself with these prophetic lyrics from Echo & the Bunnymen, 'Nothing ever lasts forever'."
David J.B. Smith (Military Author – Plymouth)

"It was truly emotional on the day of demolition."
Sharon Stoneman (St Austell, Cornwall)

"Gone but not forgotten."
Natalie Hobman (Callington, Cornwall)

"It certainly was an iconic place, sadly missed."
Tracey Lander (Bodmin, Cornwall)

"I miss the Coliseum!!"
Anonymous (Cornwall)

"Fantastic venue in its day and a very sad loss."
Sue Williams (Ulley, Sheffield)

"Such a shame an iconic venue is no more and that my son won't enjoy time there like I did.
Cornwall Coliseum will live on in our hearts forever."
Richard Ruse (St Austell, Cornwall)

"Many great memories as a teenager, Friday night roller disco, taking pennies up to the arcade, Quasars "nightclub of the nineties" - an icon that will be sadly missed."
Alison Pearson (Nr Exeter, Devon)

"I was very disappointed when it was pulled down.
What a shame the whole area has been totally ruined."
Les Deacon (Tresillian, Cornwall)

"Lovely place ....miss it."
Patricia Darch (St Austell, Cornwall)

"Loved the place such a shame being knocked down some very good memories there."
Melanie Finch (Liskeard, Cornwall)

"It's very sad to hear of venues that are lost to us but I'll always have the memories, no matter how faded.
Cornwall Coliseum... Gone but never forgotten..."
Theo Christian (Gateshead)

"Such a shame it has gone."
Jenny Wilson (Cornwall)

"To summarise

Best bits about the Colly

1. *It attracted bands and artist of all sizes.*
2. *Had a decent long bar, that you still could see the artist while being-served.*

3. *Reasonable prices in Wimpy.*
4. *Free to park / Large car park at front and rear of complex.*
5. *Great load in area. Straight from back of lorry to stage.*
6. *Good outdoor pool, and children's amusement area.*
7. *Close enough to Plymouth, so didn`t have to travel hundred of miles to see artist*
8. *The Munchkins*
9. *Gossips Nightclub*
10. *Radio 1 Roadshow*

Worse Bits

1. *Queue to get out of the car park and up the hill.*
2. *The pillar.*
3. **Its Gone...**
   # John Lintern (Plymouth, Devon)

Other Books Available
By Ian Carroll

Horror Books

The Lovers Guide To Internet Dating

Demon Pirates Vs Vikings

Valentines Day

My Name Is Ishmael

A-Z of Bloody Horror 'A' is for 'Antique Shop'

A-Z of Bloody Horror 'M' is for 'Warning: Water May Contain Mermaids'

Music Books

The Reading Festival: Music, Mud and Mayhem – available in full version or as 1970's, 1980's and 1990's

From Donington to Download – available in full version or as 'Monsters of Rock' and 'Download Festival'

King 810 – an introduction to the band

All available on Amazon on Kindle and in Paperback for a bargain price

Printed in Great Britain
by Amazon.co.uk, Ltd.,
Marston Gate.